AF223833

THE ABC'S OF MARRIAGE

Before and After You Say I Do

DANA JAMES

Copyright © 2021 Dana James
All rights reserved.
ISBN TP:978-1-7359689-0-2
ISBN eBook:978-1-7359689-1-9

Divine Destiny Publishers, LLC
Owings Mills, MD 21117
Editing & Proofreading by Grammargal
Cover design by Wotbdesigns and Jamar Hargrove
Reach us at: www.divinedestinypublishers.com

This book is dedicated to all those who are in relationships or desire to be in relationships. Always remember relationships take work, but never lose sight of the fact that you matter, your dreams matter, and your destiny matters. Don't compromise and don't settle. Wait for that special person God has for you who will help you shine. If you are married, always remember, the little things matter.

FOREWORD
LENIKA SCOTT
The Millionaire Mom

It was certainly an honor and a privilege to be called upon to write this book foreword. I've had the pleasure of working with Dana James during times of business and spiritual coaching. One of the things I love about Dana is she is an executor! She implements and executes well, and it is no surprise she has executed an excellent read! Dana James is a woman after God's own heart who has written a book based upon foundational truths about marriage.

Marriage is no easy feat; ask me how I know! I've been married for twenty-five years (and counting) and birthed six daughters over a span of twelve years. I understand firsthand the many ups and downs and the many rewards that can come from two individuals who are determined to make it work. The marriages that last are built on a solid foundation in Christ and also proven principles. Many of these principles are discussed in this book.

The ABC's of Marriage is a powerful book that all couples need to read. So whether you are dating, have plans of entering into marriage, or have been married, you need this book.

A short yet impactful read highlighting essential areas that need to be addressed in relationships, each chapter features the letter of the alphabet with a word that coincides with the area of focus. For example, the letter C - Compassion. After each word is defined, Dana shares a personal story that validates why she is qualified to write on this subject.

I believe her transparency in this book will give readers hope and assurance that they are not the only ones facing battles that can be won by the grace of God. I also believe her transparency will bring forth healing to many.

What I also love about *The ABC's of Marriage* is it ends with a prayer and even a suggested area for the reader to take actionable steps that can improve the relationship.

This book will also cause you to quickly recognize if you have fallen into a place of relationship drought or areas you need to deal with as a person. When we are broken as individuals, make no mistake about it, it affects our relationships. It's time to heal!

If you need refreshing in your marriage, (especially) if things have gotten dry or dull, please allow the pages in this book not only minister to your heart but also challenge you to do better.

You deserve the best!

CONTENTS

CHAPTER ONE
A - ACRIMONY

bitterness or ill feeling

It may seem strange that acrimony is the first word of the alphabet. All relationships go through ups and downs. Sometimes there are intense downs. There are hurts that can take you to a level of anger that is totally out of character for you. Because we are all human, we tend to allow our emotions to take a front seat to our mind and our will and lead our spirit man down a path we would not normally go.

As the definition says, *acrimony* is "bitterness, resentment, ill feeling, and finger-pointing." You know those days that you have a disagreement with your spouse or your significant other and you begin to feel all these emotions, and all of a sudden, the finger-pointing begins. "It's all his fault." "If he had just listened to me . . ." "If she had not made that decision without asking me first, we wouldn't be where we are now." Did you just see what that last sentence said? "If she had only asked me first." Relationships are hard enough as it is without one of us telling or insisting that the other ask before they do something.

When you are in a relationship, there are times where both of you need to bend. Bending does not mean that you must give in; it simply means that you are always open to hearing what the other person is saying and coming to an agreement to make something happen. Never use the statement, "Did you ask me?" or "I told you to . . ." These are surefire triggers to cause arguments. When these statements are used, the person receiving them goes on the defensive. Whether it's verbally or silently, it opens a whole can of worms that doesn't need to be opened. That's when true acrimony comes forth, and in return you get, "You're not my mother/father. I'm grown, and you don't tell me what to do!"

We have to remember that words are powerful, and as the Bible says in Proverbs 18:21, "The tongue has the power of life and death, and those who love it will eat its fruit."

I remember a time in my marriage where I dealt with my spouse's infidelity. It was something that I never thought would happen to me. I thought I would have the perfect marriage. I thought my husband would love me just as much as I loved him. That was not so. This was the first time I experienced true anger, animosity, hostility, and, yes, even spite.

First, I got the feeling that something wasn't right because there was a distance between us. The communication basically stopped, and there was a lack of attention to me, which meant his needs were not being met. I began watching and listening for any signs, large or small. He would disappear for long periods of time and come home offering no explanation of where he had been. The phone would ring, and he would begin to speak in code. God gave me the spirit of discernment, and all I had to do was let it kick in. I knew what was going on in my heart and in my spirit. I just didn't have any proof. I did everything I knew to save my marriage. I cried alone, I cried to God and with Him, and I did a whole lot of praying. I also did a lot of asking Him what I did to deserve this. I've always tried to treat people the way I wanted them to treat me. I gave him all I knew to give. What more did he want? I forgave and forgave and forgave until I realized that I wasn't as important as the other woman. That was my wake-up call.

Often in relationships we find ourselves giving all we are and all we have to the other person and getting lost in the process. We forget who we are and Whose we are in the process. We are children of the Most High God (Ps. 82:6). The Bible also tells us in Deuteronomy 28:13 (NIV), "The LORD will make you the head, not the tail. If you pay attention to the commands of the LORD your God that I give you this day and carefully follow them, you will always be at the top, never at the bottom." This is what the Bible says about marriage in Ephesians 5:25 (KJV), "For husbands, this means love your wives, just as Christ loved the church, and gave himself up his life for it." This only applies to those of us who know God and live our lives according to His instructions (the Bible). We can't hold our partners accountable if they are not walking with Him. This is where being "equally yoked" (Cor. 6:14) comes into play. Genesis 2:24 (ESV) says: "Therefore a man shall leave his father and his mother and hold fast to his wife, and they shall become one flesh."

Second Corinthians 6:14 (AMP) tells us: "Do not be unequally bound together with unbelievers [do not make mismatched alliances with them, inconsistent with your faith]. For what partnership can righteousness have with lawlessness? Or what fellowship can light have with darkness?" Most of the time we make the decision of who to marry or get into a relationship with without asking God for His guidance and direction. Our parents do all they can to protect us from hurt and going down a road that will only cause us pain. God our Father does the same thing. He has our best interest at heart. All we have to do is listen and allow Him to guide us through the journey of love.

Ultimately, I made the hardest decision I've ever made in my life. But it only came after I listened to my Heavenly Father and allowed Him to guide and lead me. I yielded my will to His will. I realized that I was important and that I was loved by Him. I didn't know how to love myself, which is why I always seemed to get in relationships that didn't have my best interest at heart. I learned that each day I have to speak life to myself. I continually told myself who God said I was and what I had a right to. He says in Deuteronomy 28:13 (NIV), "The Lord will make you the head, not the tail. If you pay attention to the commands of the Lord your God that I give you this day and carefully follow them, you will always be at the top, never at the bottom." I am loved, the hardening of my mind has been removed in Christ (Gal. 3:28), God supplies all my needs (Phil. 4:19), and He chose me (1 Thes. 1:4)!

I didn't allow acrimony to rule my life and take control. I took back the power and authority that my Father gave me. It wasn't an easy road, but it was one that I had to travel to become the person I was destined to be. Never give up on you, even when it looks like you are traveling alone—and sometimes you are. There are times when the journey you are on is one that no one can take with you. Sometimes you must learn to be alone with yourself, to love yourself, to even like yourself. You may need to learn your importance to yourself and to others. You will also have to learn that ultimately you are never alone because God is always with you, holding you, lifting you up, catching you when you fall, and loving you through it all.

Acrimony will not defeat you. It is only a stepping stone to your greater destiny.

The LORD your God is with you, the Mighty Warrior who saves. He will take great delight in you; in his love he will no longer rebuke you, but will rejoice over you with singing.
(Zeph. 3:17 ESV)

Dana's prayer:

God, I come to you thanking you for always being my guide and leading me even when I feel as if I am all alone. Thank you for covering my mind, body, soul, and spirit. God, I pray that you give me the desire and the strength to release all ill will, bitterness, hostility, and anger toward people who have hurt me to my core. I ask that you guard my heart and my mind so that I don't lose who I am in the process of this journey and that I don't stay stuck where I am. God, I desire to be free and in line with what you have planned for my life on this journey to my destiny. I thank you, and I bless your Holy name! Amen.

What are your takeaways?

____

____

____

____

____

____

____

How can you use this to move toward your destiny?

____

____

____

____

____

____

____

Your prayer:

____

____

____

CHAPTER TWO

B - BROKEN/BROKENNESS

forcibly separated into two or more pieces;
fractured

____

When we go into relationships, we bring a ton of baggage with us. Bags and boxes that we've carried with us from relationship to relationship. Some of them we haven't even looked into since we packed them. What's in the bags and boxes? All of the things that caused us to be broken. All the circumstances that we have allowed us to be stuck, crippled, and unable to move toward our true destiny. For many years I carried my bags and boxes with me from relationship to relationship. Everything in those bags has contributed to my brokenness.

As a child, I was molested by my babysitter's son. I was also a compulsive liar, so I felt no one would believe me. Remember the story about the boy who cried wolf too many times? At the age of seven, I felt like that boy, and that no one would believe me. I think that was the first box I ever packed. The box remained packed until I was in my late forties. I am now fifty-three. This is the first time my power was taken from me. My way of keeping the pieces I still had together was to pack away the hurt, the anger, the shame, the bitterness, the feeling of being unclean and unworthy. I put tape on the box and put the broken pieces of my life on the shelf. I didn't have anything to hide the box behind, so it was always in the front of my mind.

I began picking up other things to try to replace the broken pieces I had put in the box. I think the first thing I picked up was a smile. I didn't realize before this very moment that's why I smile so much. I believe I put it on and used it as a mask, to hide the brokenness that would be shown on my face if I didn't cover it up. No matter how I felt or where I went, I always wore my mask. If it didn't make me feel better, at least it would bring joy to other people I came in contact with. Tonya Joyner-Scott would consider this part of being a "recovering people pleaser." Everything I did was to ensure that everyone was taken care of even if it meant that I wasn't.

Another box I packed and traveled with for many years was the box that contained lies and deception. These pieces came from relationships where I had been lied to by the men in my life and the actions and consequences that came from those situations. I picked up the pieces of my broken life after finding out that the man I was seeing had been seeing someone else at the same time he was dating me. I also found out that the other woman was pregnant and that they were getting married. He didn't tell me; I learned it from general conversation with someone else. You see, again, my spiritual antenna went up. I felt it, but in your heart and mind you don't really want to believe that a special person would lie to you and cheat on you. I pulled my dustpan and broom out and began to sweep the broken pieces into a brand-new box. Once I finished, I taped it up and put it on the shelf.

As a result of being broken time and time again, I began to feel less than I knew God said I was. I felt unworthy and unloved. I also began to wonder what was wrong with me. Why couldn't a man love me unconditionally the way God says he should (Eph. 5:25 NIV): "Husbands, love your wives, as Christ loved the church and gave himself up for her." I thought for sure I would be loved and cared for this way when I got married, but I wasn't.

Many times one spouse feels as if they are giving 150 percent but they are only getting 50 percent. This also causes more broken pieces. I got tired of carrying all those bags and boxes around with me everywhere I went. I got tired of wearing that mask even when I didn't feel like it. I had prayed and cried out to God. He was speaking, but I couldn't hear him because I was still stuck on all those things I had packed away in those boxes. God told me to open those boxes and go through everything in them. He said in Ephesians 4:31-32 (ESV): "Let all bitterness and wrath and anger and clamor and slander be put away from you, along with malice. Be kind to one another, tenderhearted, forgiving one another, as God in Christ forgave you." I learned that in order for me to be free, I had to forgive all those people who had hurt me.

Many times we go through life harboring ill feelings toward people who hurt us ten and twenty years ago. Guess what? Those people have moved on and don't even remember what they did to hurt you. They are walking around happy-go-lucky, and you are walking around sick physically, mentally, and spiritually. Only when you forgive them can you truly begin to allow God to fix the broken pieces of your life. God will replace those pieces with some amazing things. He made you a masterpiece (Eph. 2:10): "For we are God's masterpiece. He has created us anew in Christ Jesus, so we can do the good things he planned for us long ago." Let go of all those things holding you back. We must take the limits off Him (Eph. 3:2): "Now to Him who is able to do exceedingly abundantly above all that we ask or think, according to the power that works in us."

Brokenness is not your portion.

Trust in the Lord with all your heart, and do not lean on your own understanding. In all your ways acknowledge him, and he will make straight your paths. (Prov. 3:5-6)

• • •

Dana's prayer:

Father God, I thank you for this new day in you. I pray that every person who has been broken and has been holding on to the boxes and luggage filled with the broken pieces of their lives will pull the boxes down off the shelf right now. I pray that they will hear your voice as they begin to unpack all the hurt, pain, hang-ups, and everything that has kept them in the place called "stuck." I thank you right now for the new pieces you are replacing within them as they begin to forgive and let go of bitterness, resentment, low self-esteem, and anything else that is not from you. I give you praise for the new beginnings in their lives, in Jesus's name, Amen.

What are your takeaways?

____

____

____

____

____

____

____

How can you use this to move toward your destiny?

____

____

____

____

____

____

____

• • •

Your prayer:

CHAPTER THREE
C - COMPASSION

embodies a tangible expression of love for
those who are suffering, kindness

God uses relationships to test us, to see if we are able to handle what He has orchestrated for our lives. Marriage is full of many things that will push you to what seem to be your limits. Sometimes you feel like you are going to lose your mind and become a person who is out of character for you. All of these scenarios bring us to compassion.

I've found myself in relationships where I've been pushed to the edge and I didn't know if I'd be able to come back. I was engaged to someone who was controlling mentally and emotionally. Subconsciously, I knew if I didn't get out it could turn to physical abuse. You can't go into a relationship holding on to things and people that have hurt you. You are bringing all that negativity into your new relationship. You must be let go of all the hurt, anger, pain, and shame. You must learn to love yourself before you can give love to someone else. I know it's hard for women and men who have been abused to let people get too close to them. Your guard is always up. When God created Adam, He didn't want him to be alone, so He put him to sleep and performed surgery. He took a rib from Adam and created Eve, his true soulmate. God has someone out there for each and every one of us, but we must open ourselves up and allow people in. We can't let them in until we come to the realization that we have issues we need to work through.

For many years after my divorce I didn't let any men in. Once I had gone through a period of working on me, I felt I was ready to take a chance and allow someone into my heart space. I was engaged to a man I thought was going to be my knight in shining armor. I saw him as kind, handsome, and loving. He would drop me off at work and pick me up in the evening in my car. He was always there. I thought that was great. That was what I had always envisioned my relationship would be. Until one night, I was driving back at about 1:30 a.m. from a movie premiere with my sorority sisters at BET in Washington, DC. I felt as if someone was following me, so I began to switch lanes and watch the other car in my rearview mirror. Sure enough, I was being followed. I became a bit unsettled and got ready to call my cousin who wasn't far away, to have him on standby because I was on my way. Before I could make the call, my fiancé called me to check on me and see where I was. I told him, and as the conversation went on, I realized that he was the one following me. I finally got him to admit that it was him. He thought it was funny. He said he had to make sure I was okay, so he basically stalked me. The hairs on the back of my neck stood up, but I didn't really want to see it as stalking.

He became controlling and manipulative, always taking me where I needed to go and wanting to listen to my conversations. Then one day he called me and told me he had been arrested for not paying child support. I went to the jail the following day to visit him and to see what needed to be done to get him out. I learned how much it would cost and began trying to pull the money together. I took money from as many places as I could until I was all out of options. We were having a family meeting, and I had to tell my family what was going on in hopes that they would be able to help me come up with the rest of the money. They immediately began putting money in to make up the difference. What I didn't know at the time was that they didn't really care too much for him, but because they loved me unconditionally as God shows us in John 3:16, they helped me help him in spite of how they felt. Sometimes we are afraid to ask for help because we are afraid we will be turned down. James 4:2 says, "You have not because you ask not." The people who truly love you will tell you the truth and help you at the same time. God has put them in our lives to guide us and speak into our lives even if we don't want to hear what they have to say at the moment.

As time went on and I prepared for the wedding, I grew more uncomfortable in my spirit. I knew this whole situation wasn't right. The final straw was when I learned that my son really didn't like him. At that point I realized that I had to put a stop to the relationship. It was one thing for me to have given my mind, body, and soul to this man, but to put my child in a potentially volatile situation was not acceptable. I knew I had to get free of him. I prayed and asked God how I was going to break this engagement. What was everyone going to say and think? Again, I was more concerned about what others thought instead of my safety and the safety of my child. He never put his hands on me, but I allowed him to control every aspect of my life. I was afraid that physical control would be next. I finally mustered up enough strength to break off the engagement. I took back my freedom!

Again, I needed to be delivered from that situation. I cried out and prayed for God to help me. He told me that he did. Until I could see that, I would not be fully delivered. Isaiah 43:18-19 (NIV) says: "Forget the former things; do not dwell on the past. See, I am doing a new thing! Now it springs up; do you not perceive it? I am making a way in the wilderness and streams in the wasteland." In spite of the situation, God did a new thing in me, and from it I gained strength and freedom.

So no matter what you are going through and no matter how it looks, know that God is there and He has your back. Psalm 23:5

(NIV): "You prepare a table before me in the presence of my enemies. You anoint my head with oil. My cup runs over."

Deliverance is your portion!

He said: "The LORD is my rock, my fortress and my deliverer; my God is my rock, in whom I take refuge, my shield and the horn of my salvation. He is my stronghold, my refuge and my savior— from violent people you save me." (2 Sam. 22:2-3 NIV)

Dana's prayer:

God, I come to you asking that you deliver everyone who has a desire to be closer to you. I pray that they will let go of all the things that have held them back from the promises you have spoken to them. I also pray that they release all people, situations, and things that have distracted them from your ultimate goal for them. True deliverance and freedom. In Jesus's name, Amen.

Assignment:

When was the last time you showed compassion to someone? The first thing is to show compassion to yourself. Take a minute and forgive yourself for falling short of a goal you didn't reach. It's okay. Just start over from where you left off and head for the finish line. We are all human and fall short sometimes. If you are not so hard on yourself, you won't be so hard on others.

What are your takeaways?

____

____

____

____

____

____

____

How can you use this to move toward your destiny?

____

____

____

____

____

____

____

Your prayer:

____

____

____

____

____

____

____

CHAPTER FOUR
D - DELIVERED
to hand over, to set free, surrender

After my childhood period as a bully, being punished almost every day for doing things I knew were wrong for attention, and months of sexual abuse, I decided that I couldn't take it any longer. At seven, I felt my only way out was to take my life. I got a bottle of baby aspirin, went into my room, and closed the door. Before going to sleep for the night, I ate the entire bottle of pills and lay down in my bed believing that this was the end and I would no longer have to suffer. The next morning, I woke up as usual. I was disappointed because I knew that the abuse would continue because I didn't have the power to fight back. I was seven and he was nineteen. I cried and told God I was sorry and asked for Him to forgive me. That was the day I was delivered and set free. I couldn't see the light at the end of the tunnel, but I remembered the things my grandparents taught me in our home Bible studies and things I had heard in church. I believed that better was in store for me.

. . .

One of the things that I developed due to my childhood molestation was a spirit of promiscuity. I'm still not sure if it manifested because I felt I deserved it or because of the things I had. I found myself t a young age having sex because the boys told me they loved me. What did we know about love? Nothing. I still had the same feeling of emptiness I had after being molested time and time again.

When I went away to college, I was so excited because I'd never been away from home I thought to myself, I'd finally be free to do anything I wanted. I began drinking. I was seeing two guys at the same time. I thought I was grown, and this is what grown people did.

One night, my friends and I went to a party at the student union. Shortly after arriving, another female student and her friends approached me. She accused me of messing around with her boyfriend. I asked her who her boyfriend was. It turned out that her boyfriend was a young man whose mom was a friend of my aunt. She'd put me in touch with them so that I wouldn't be there alone, and they could look out for me.

After finding this out, I said to her, "I didn't know he had a girlfriend since he never mentioned you. I also told her that if I wanted him, I could have him." She proceeded to get in my face. Mind you; I had been drinking. I had a bottle of Brass Monkey before coming to the party. When she got in my face, it was as if someone had turned on a light switch. I went from calm, cool, collective Dana to ok, so you want to fight Dana. My friends who were with me saw my reaction and immediately pushed me out of the student union. The alcohol was doing all the talking for me.

As we were at the light on Beatties Ford Road going back to the dorm, this chick and her friends followed us. They followed us into the dorm as if she wanted smoke with me. She was the size of a toothpick, and I wasn't a fighter, but I was ready that night. I told her that her problem wasn't with me but with her boyfriend and that she needed to chat with him.

The next morning, I had the biggest hangover, and I had to ask my friends if what I thought happened actually happened. They said yes. After that day, I decided that drinking was not for me. I was crazy enough without it, and I didn't need any more help.

I also concluded that I wasn't getting anything out of these toxic relationships. I thought long and hard about the promiscuity and decided it wasn't worth it. By stopping these things, I was taking control back from the enemy. I had given the devil a foothold (Ephe 4:27). The power that I had voluntarily given to him, I decided to take back. I was delivered.

(Luke 10:19 NIV) "I have given you authority to trample on snakes and scorpions and to overcome all the power of the enemy; nothing will harm you."

He said: "The LORD is my rock, my fortress and my deliverer; my God is my rock, in whom I take refuge, my shield and the horn of my salvation. He is my stronghold, my refuge and my savior—from violent people you save me."
(2 Sam. 22:2-3 NIV)

Dana's prayer:
God, I come to you asking that you deliver everyone who has a desire to be closer to you. I pray that they will let go of all the things that have held them back from the promises you have spoken to them. I also pray that they release all people, situations, and things that have distracted them from your ultimate goal for them. That they take back what they have voluntarily given the enemy. True deliverance and freedom is their portion. In Jesus's name. Amen.

Assignment:
Is there something you are holding on to that you need to let go?

Search yourself and be honest. We have a tendency to lie to ourselves. Confront it and let it go. Your future depends on it.

What are your takeaways?

____

____

____

____

____

____

How can you use this to move toward your destiny?

____

____

____

____

____

____

Your prayer:

____

____

____

____

____

____

CHAPTER FIVE
E - EXPECTATIONS

a strong belief that something will happen or
be the case in the future.

Growing up, little girls have expectations about what marriage will be. We see our parents' relationships, not really thinking that their relationships will mold our relationships in the future. I think I believed the fairy tales about forever after, that everything would be great after saying, "I do." What I didn't realize was that those two words won't change anything. The way things are now are the way they will be tomorrow.

I had expectations that we would talk every day about what happened to us during the day. We would share our experiences. We would listen to each other and offer solutions and encouragement when needed. We would be open to hearing each other. These things didn't happen. I was living in a fairy tale. Part of the reason was that I had not learned to communicate. Because of some things that happened to me as a child, I kept that part of me inside. As a result, I didn't ask, "How was your day?" and if I did, I didn't get an answer, or I got one-word responses, which pretty much ended the conversation. I lived with my spouse but felt as if I was living alone.

After years of healing and deliverance, worshiping God and learning His voice, I heard Him tell me to make a list of all the things I desired in a mate. I got my notebook out and began writing my list. At the very top of the page I wrote, "God, please allow me to add to this list." I knew that He had so much in store for me and that I needed to be open to hear what he had to say. Psalms 37:4-5 (KJV): "Delight yourself also in the Lord, and He shall give you the desires of your heart. Commit your way to the Lord, trust also in Him, and He shall bring it to pass."

What I didn't know was that someone from my church was interested in me. Quite a few people at the church were in on the matchmaking, from the pastor down, but I was clueless. His friend gave him a suit to wear to my son's surprise engagement dinner. I hadn't invited him originally, but some of his friends asked if he could come, and I said sure since he was friends with my son. I didn't know what was going on until I was leaving and he pulled up and gave me candy and flowers and said, "Happy Valentine's Day and happy birthday." I didn't quite know what to say except, "Thank you." I wasn't looking at him in that way at the time. My reaction was not what he expected.

On Father's Day, the women at my church decided to have breakfast to celebrate their husbands. My co-pastor asked if I would assist her in preparing the food, and of course I said yes. At the time I had been talking to one of the men at church. She suggested that I write something for him. I was not really thinking too much about it since it was Father's Day and he was a father. I agreed. When the time came to present things to the men, she got up and said that she found this poem on the refrigerator and she wasn't quite sure who it was for. So the man I had been talking to was supposed to get up at that moment and come up to the front. She said it several times, and he never moved. I didn't realize what was going on right away, and then the Holy Spirit said, "He's going to propose." I thought to myself, "Okay . . ."

He finally got the message and walked to the front of the room with an air cast on his foot. Music began to play, and he asked me to come to the front. He then got on one knee and asked me to marry him. I said yes. What I didn't learn until later was that while I had been compiling my list of characteristics I desired in a husband, he had been praying to God for a wife. He said that every time he prayed that prayer, he saw my face. One Sunday morning, I was at the light making a left on my way to church and he was at the light to the right of me going straight. (I didn't see him, but he saw me.) He said he had just prayed to God about his wife and looked over and there I was.

We both had expectations of what we wanted in our mates, and we included God in the process. When you are open to receiving God's best for you, it will come when you least expect it in ways you never would have imagined. You never know who's watching you.

Expect God's best for your life!

"For I know the plans I have for you," declares the Lord, "plans to prosper you and not to harm you, plans to give you hope and a future." (Jer. 29:11 NIV)

Dana's prayer:

Father, I pray right now that your people are expecting all you have for them. I pray that their eyes, ears, hearts, and minds are open to see all that you have placed before them. I also pray that they are open to the fact that "no" doesn't always mean "never" but that it can mean "not right now." I pray that they will learn to be patient as they wait in anticipation but also remember that they have to do something during the waiting process. Thank you, God, Amen.

. . .

Assignment:

1. What are you looking for in a relationship?

2. Write down what you desire in a mate. No matter how big or small, add it to your list, and remember that you can add to it at any time.

What are your takeaways?

____

____

____

____

____

____

____

How can you use this to move toward your destiny?

____

____

____

____

____

____

Your prayer?

____

____

____

CHAPTER SIX

F - FEAR, FAITH, FORGIVENESS

awareness of danger; complete trust; to stop
feeling angry or resentful toward someone for
an offense, flaw, or mistake

I find myself coming back to the events that happened to me as a child. The molestation. I've learned over the years that this was key in making me the person I am today. Some aspects of it are positive, while others are not. They have hindered my growth, caused me to live in fear of certain things. I've found myself fearful in my relationships, fearful that I would fail, and even fearful of succeeding. I never knew that type of fear existed.

So first, let's look at my fear as it relates to relationships. I've been afraid that I'm not pretty enough, not desirable. Let's be real, I'm human, and everyone wants and needs to feel desired. I've been fearful of saying the wrong things. I've felt that if I said the wrong thing, the person I was with would leave me. Sometimes I've even found myself dumbing myself down so the other person in the relationship would feel they were in control. Another result of being fearful is relinquishing who I am to the other person. I've basically given them my power. I've allowed them to tell me what to do, when to do it, and how to do it. I've even allowed someone to listen to a conversation with a long-time male friend so he could make sure it wasn't a booty call. It all seems crazy now looking back and seeing how much of my power I gave away to men I was in relationships with. That whole situation with the fiancé trying to confirm I wasn't lying about the booty call should have been a red flag to me, but again, I was living in fear.

One night after watching my cousin while his parents were out, I started to feel funny. I went to the restroom and saw blood. I had not gone to the doctor prior to that day but knew in my mind that I was pregnant. I was afraid to tell the father that I was pregnant. The cramping got worse, so I left the house and immediately went to the hospital. I got confirmation that I was pregnant and that I was losing the baby. After leaving the hospital, I called the father to let him know what was going on, and his reaction shocked me. I'm not sure why it did. I'd been through so much with him, but I'd hoped for some compassion. I got none. That ended any thought I had of ever getting with him again.

God tells us that we are worthy, that we are children of the King, that we are heirs and joint heirs (Rom. 8:16-17). If my daddy is the King, why am I taking all this mess? He has given me the power and authority to take back everything the enemy has taken from me (Luke 10:19). It's time to tell the enemy that I am taking it all back! I want everything God has for me.

A part of my healing process was going through spiritual warfare. I was on a mission to break all generational and ancestral curses. I went through healing and deliverance. In order for me to move on from the childhood trauma, I had to confront what happened and forgive the person who stole my childhood. It is absolutely critical that we forgive those who have hurt us, so we can be free. Holding on to the anger doesn't hurt the person who hurt you. It only affects you. When we hold on to unforgiveness or anger toward someone, we aren't hurting anyone but ourselves. The person we are harboring the ill feelings for has moved on and may not even remember what they did or said to offend or hurt you, but you are still walking around with a spirit of heaviness and sickness.

The most important person to forgive is yourself. You can't forgive anyone else if you can't forgive yourself. We tend to hold ourselves hostage and blame ourselves for things that have happened to us. Those of us who have been through sexual abuse may blame ourselves for what happened to us. I blamed myself because as a child I lied to my parents, stole, and was a bully. My seven-year-old rationale was that had I not done those things, my "friend" wouldn't have been able to blackmail me into the sexual abuse. I had to learn to release myself from that guilt because it wasn't my fault and I didn't deserve it no matter what I had done. Just remember that God has better for you just have faith. "Be kind to one another, tenderhearted, forgiving one another, as God in Christ forgave you" (Eph. 4:32 NIV). "And whenever you stand praying, forgive, if you have anything against anyone, so that your Father also who is in heaven may forgive you your trespasses (Mark 11:25 KJV)."

Forgiveness: giving up my right to hurt you for hurting me. To wipe the slate clean, to pardon, to cancel a debt.

Most of my life I lived with the memory of sexual abuse from my childhood. I learned many years later that there were things I needed to do in order to be totally free from it. The main thing was to forgive the person who abused me. I didn't know where to start.

My pastors announced that they were taking the church through inner healing and deliverance. This was the first time I told anyone about my abuse. I remember crying uncontrollably, shaking, and lying on the floor in the fetal position. I remember feeling the pain, anger, and hurt rising up inside me. All I wanted was to be free, to be able to have a normal relationship with my husband. I didn't realize at the time that the abuse had an effect on how I viewed myself and how I interacted with my husband.

I cried out to God asking Him again why this happened to me. I told Him that I wanted to be free. I didn't want to carry this inside any longer. I needed to release it because it was holding me back in so many areas of my life. Jesus loved me so much that he paid the price for my emotional healing on the cross. Isaiah 53:4 says, "Surely he took up our pain . . . yet we considered him punished by God." I had to learn that in order for my soul to be free, I had to give all of it over to Jesus as it says in Matthew 11:28-30 (NIV), "Come to me, all you who are weary and burdened, and I will give you rest. Take my yoke upon you and learn from me, for I am gentle and humble in heart, and you will find rest for your souls. For my yoke is easy and my burden is light."

I needed to tell him that I forgave him and myself so I could be free. Unconsciously I had been blaming myself for what happened to me. I thought it wouldn't have happened to me if I hadn't done all the lying, stealing, and bullying I had done. I learned that it wasn't my fault and that no one deserves to have that happen to them. There is nothing I did to deserve it. Once I released myself, I needed to release him. Since I didn't know where he was, I had to release him verbally. I had to verbally speak and say that I forgave him for taking away my innocence and for making me do things that no child should have to endure. One thing about forgiveness is that when you go to the person you are forgiving or the person you want to forgive you, you must be specific. You can't just go and say, "John, please forgive me for what I did to you." That isn't telling what you are asking or giving forgiveness for. You should say something like this, "John, please forgive me for arguing with you and pushing you last year on the Fourth of July. I didn't mean to. I wasn't mad at you. I was going through something at home and took my frustration out on you. Please forgive me." They may not even remember what you are talking about, which is another reason you must be specific. Once you have gone to them, God will say, "Well done."

I think one of the definitions of forgiveness is so powerful:

"giving up my right to hurt you for hurting me." What an awesome world this would be if we all lived by that. God desires us to live lives free of hurt, pain, anger, bitterness, and the spirit of vengeance. Deuteronomy 32:35 (NIV) says, "It is mine to avenge; I will repay. In due time their foot will slip; their day of disaster is near, and their doom rushes upon them."

Forgiveness removes those things that prevent God's ability to bless you and move you closer to your destiny.

Be kind and compassionate to one another, forgiving each other, just as in Christ God forgave you. (Eph. 4:32 NIV)

Dana's prayer:

Father, in the name of Jesus, I come to you today giving you glory, honor, and praise. God, I thank you for covering and protecting all your children. I pray right now in the matchless name of Jesus against the tactics of the enemy to keep your children bound by the spirit of fear. God, I pray right now that it is broken in Jesus's name! I also pray that your children are free from fear in their minds. I decree and declare that the fear traumas they have been holding to are replaced with faith in Jesus's name. I decree and declare that they will no longer hold themselves hostage by what happened to them, that they are now free in the name of Jesus. I thank you for allowing us to forgive ourselves. I pray that your children feel your peace and your presence right now as freedom overtakes them. I decree and declare that they are now free to walk in their destiny and that all doors that were closed as a result of the experiences of the past are now open for them to walk through with faith, freedom, and boldness. I pray that they remember daily that they are blessed, that their Father does not condemn them and that He has their backs in Jesus's name. I also come to you because I choose to forgive the person who has wronged me. I release them, and I set myself free. I pray that your healing will overtake me. I will no longer be stuck in the situation or continue to talk about it. Father, I thank You for forgiving me as I forgive them. Thank you for releasing me. In Jesus's name, Amen.

Now walk into your destiny with the power and authority God has given you!

Assignment:

1. Look back over the years to determine if there is someone you've been holding unforgiveness toward. If there is, you need to release them. If the person is still living, go to them and let them know that you forgive them for *a*, *b*, *c*, and *d*. Be specific. Remember, the forgiveness is not for them; it's for you.

2. Don't allow fear to hold you back or hinder you from moving forward. Examine yourself. Is there something you're afraid of doing or afraid of not doing? You can accomplish anything! Have faith.

What are your takeaways?

____

____

____

____

____

____

____

How can you use this to move toward your destiny?

____

Your prayer:

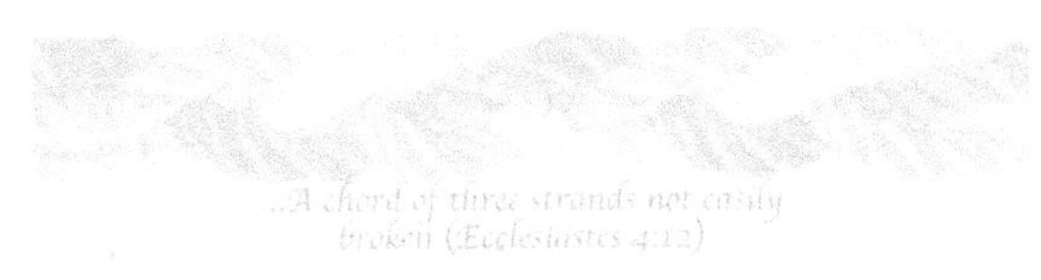

CHAPTER SEVEN
G - GIVING

providing love or other emotional support;
caring.

All relationships require giving and taking. There are times in the relationship where each person feels that they are giving more than they are getting. This can cause them to feel heavy, disconnected from the relationship, and like they want to give up. They feel that they are not getting as much love as they are giving, or that they are not being supported emotionally.

There are times when you may come home after a rough day, and you want to vent to your spouse about what happened, and you hope they will listen and give you some type of feedback. All you want is for them to acknowledge that you had a rough day and to give you some encouragement that everything will be okay, even if they don't understand what you do. If they topped it off with a hug, that would lift all heaviness. Instead of getting that, you don't get any response or even an acknowledgment that you were even having a conversation. This type of situation causes you to shut down and keep things to yourself, and that's not good for you physically or mentally. Everyone needs a sounding board. Genesis 2:18 (NIV) says, "The Lord God said, it is not good for man to be alone. I will make a helper suitable for him."

Marriage should allow you to grow closer and not further apart. We must learn to stop and take time out for each other. Have a family meeting and decide that each day you will sit down as a family and have dinner together. That is what our parents and grandparents used to do. Everyone had to be home by a certain time, and dinner was on the table. That was a time for everyone to share about their day and express themselves. We are so busy stopping at fast-food restaurants and having the kids eat in the car that when we get home, everyone is going in separate directions. There is a disconnect in the family, and it is our jobs as parents and spouses to put it all back in order. Proverbs 22:6 (KJV) says, "Train up a child in the way he should go; even when he is old he will not depart from it." Ecclesiastes 4:9-12 (KJV) says, "Two are better than one, because they have a good return for their labor: either of them falls down, one can help the other up. But pity anyone who falls also, and has no one to help them up. Also, if two lie down together, they will keep warm. But how can one keep warm alone? Though one may be overpowered, two can defend themselves. A cord of three strands is not quickly broken."

Family is one of the most powerful things God gave us. It's up to us to hold it together. Giving love and emotional support to your spouse and your children is key to a successful home! Take time each day to be quick to listen and slow to speak. James 1:19 (NIV) says, "My dear brothers and sisters, take note of this: Everyone should be quick to listen, slow to speak and slow to become angry." Perhaps it's time to pull out the family manual (the Bible) and follow the instructions.

God has given you wonderful gifts. Now it's time for you to give back. It's the small things that mean so much. For example, surprise your wife with flowers weekly or monthly. Wives, go out and find your husband's favorite treat and bring it to him once in a while. Parents, take the kids out to the park or the lake and walk around. You'll be amazed at the smiles on their faces, and guess what, it doesn't cost you anything but time.

. . .

Give, and it will be given to you. A good measure, pressed down, shaken together and running over, will be poured into your lap. For with the measure you use, it will be measured to you. (Luke 6:38 NIV)

Dana's prayer:

Father, I pray for all relationships and families. I pray that they will learn how to give to each other the things that each other needs. I pray they learn that it's not about material things but about things of the heart. I pray for open ears, hearts, and minds. I also pray for creative ways for them to give to each other and that they would be able to receive in Jesus's name. Remind them, Father, that they are worthy to receive because they are your children, Amen.

Assignment:

1. Come together and have conversations when one of you wants to give financially to a family member or friend. If you don't, it can cause division in your relationship. Leave no doors open for the enemy to enter.

2. Give support to each other when one has a desire to better themselves. Make sure you come together to develop a plan since the change will affect you both and your family. Remember, your choice now affects someone else.

What are your takeaways?

____

____

____

____

How can you use this to move toward your destiny?

Your prayer:

CHAPTER EIGHT

H - HUSBAND

the head of the wife as Christ is the head of
the church. A good husband loves his wife
unconditionally and is a servant leader just
like Christ.(Ephesians 5:25)

Growing up, I believed in fairy tales. I thought my husband would be my knight in shining armor that would come along and sweep me off my feet. That he would love me, protect me, and keep me safe. That we would have days filled with happiness, honesty, love, and trust. As an adult, I learned that was not the way it would be. I learned that marriage takes a lot of work.

Men have no idea how to be husbands, just as women don't truly know how to be good wives. We do have a manual called the Bible that gives us great instructions. We strive to follow them, but we are human, and sometimes the human side wins over the spiritual side. The definition seems pretty straightforward, but I think it gets lost in the process of daily life.

I've spoken to men about their wives, trying to help them understand what was going on with them. In some of my conversations I learned that the husband has relinquished his authority and given it to the wife. He's following Christ, but he's not communicating strongly enough about the things that really matter in the relationship. Usually it's money and the kids. They are on two different pages about how the finances should work and how the kids should be raised. Husbands must understand that it's not their job to control their wives, to tell them what they can and can't do, what they can and can't wear, and where they can and can't go. You two became one when you said, "I do" (Matt. 19:6).

Husbands should love their wives unconditionally. It shouldn't be based on what she does or doesn't do. It should be based on respect, and he should love her at all times (Eph. 5:25). Husbands are also supposed to make sacrifices as the head of the home. Christ was the example. He washed his disciples' feet as a demonstration to us. It's your job to make sure that your wife's emotional, spiritual, and material needs are met. Fellas, we look to you to show us the way, to make sure that we are on one page when it comes to finances. It's not the woman's position to ensure that the home is financially stable. It's your duty. This is one of the areas in which our marriages are out of order and why there is so much chaos, confusion, and discord. Finance meetings are crucial in a marriage. Come together each month and work out your plan of attack, your budget. You must tell your money where to go, or it will just go! Husbands, your wives will love you and appreciate you more for taking the lead. She won't mind paying the bills as long as you have talked about it together.

Remember to lift her up and cover her. Don't go out and tell everyone what she does that you don't like. The only person you need to talk about that with is her. When you do it, do it in love. Also, what goes on at home stays at home. If your wife dresses a certain way to ensure that she's comfortable and presentable the next morning, don't talk about her in these streets. We will cover her in a later chapter.

Husbands, lead by example, and your wife and children will follow you.

. . .

But I would have you know, that the head of every man is Christ; and the head of the woman is man; and the head of Christ is God. (1 Cor. 11:3)

Dana's prayer;

God, I come to you asking your protection over all the husbands. God, that you would cover their minds, their eye gates, their ear gates, and their spirits. Father, I pray that your angels would encamp around them when the enemy tries to knock them off of their designated path. I pray that they will only hear your voice, God, and that they will be good stewards over what you have given them authority over. I pray that they will yield to your guidance when it comes to loving and caring for their wives and children. I thank you for them, and I bless you in Jesus's name, Amen.

What are your takeaways?

____
____
____
____
____
____
____

How can you use this to move toward your destiny?

____
____
____
____
____

Your prayer:

CHAPTER NINE

I - INTIMACY AND INFIDELITY

a closeness and togetherness in a
relationship; the action or state of being
unfaithful to a spouse

God intended for marriage to be the most intimate relationship there could be. He intended for it to be the vehicle for man and woman to become one. There are several forms of intimacy in marriage.

First, there is emotional intimacy. *Emotional intimacy* means that you are open to exposing yourself emotionally to each other. You have to be open to show each other how you feel. You must be transparent and not keep things inside. You have to remember not to take advantage of the emotional part the other partner has shared with you. You should feel safe and comfortable about opening up about your feelings.

Next is physical intimacy. *Physical intimacy* is the most intimate form of becoming one just as God designed. Physical intimacy is not just about sex. It includes hugging, kissing, and holding hands. Touch communicates love, appreciation, support, concern, compassion, and understanding.

Couples also experience spiritual intimacy in marriage. God intended for us to be one all across the board. Together you have to put Christ as the center of your marriage. The Bible talks about the cord that's not easily broken. Ecclesiastes 4:12 (KJV) says, "Though one may be overpowered by another, two can withstand him. And a threefold cord is not quickly broken." You should pray for one another and together. I find myself waking up in the middle of the night, and I put my hands on my husband and begin to pray for him. I'm trying to listen to God and pray when He says to pray and move when He says to move. Daily devotional or Bible study time together allows the two of you to join as one and intimately join with God.

In our culture, we see on television and in our everyday lives that infidelity is an accepted practice. Men give other men high fives for doing it, and women are now providing each other support for doing it because their spouse did it to them. Something is wrong with this picture. In Genesis 2:24, when God established marriage between Adam and Eve, he created "one flesh" relationships.

There are many reasons for infidelity, but the main one seems to be that there is a lack of an emotional connection. We need to feel wanted, needed, and understood. One spouse may think that they are not getting emotional intimacy from their mate, so they go out and look for it someplace else. God designed sex to be enjoyable in a marriage. Hebrews 13:4 (NIV) says, "Marriage should be honored by all, and the marriage bed kept pure, for God will judge the adulterer and all the sexually immoral."

Marriages are not perfect. We can have miscommunications, arguments, and disagreements. When this happens, we may reach out to a friend or a coworker for support or another point of view. There is nothing wrong with trying to get support and feedback, but it may not be a good idea to get it from someone of the opposite sex. When you share this private information with another person, you are opening yourself up emotionally. Sharing can lead to a deeper emotional connection with the other person.

Sharing our problems or even our dreams and ambitions with someone means that we have developed a level of trust with that person. Placing trust in another person and opening up to them emotionally also makes us vulnerable.

You can begin to look at the person you're sharing the information with as more caring and supportive than your spouse. Doing this can lead to even more significant issues with your spouse.

Becoming emotionally involved with someone can lead to sexual intimacy. Although intentions may be innocent when emotional relationships are developed between opposite-sex friends, it is best to be cautious. Emotional intimacy can be a much deeper connection than sexual intimacy. Sadly, sexual relationships do not always lead to emotional intimacy, but connecting with someone emotionally first can lead to a sexual relationship.

To have a spouse be unfaithful is one of the worst feelings you could ever have. You feel alone and begin to wonder what you did wrong or even what's wrong with you. You might also ask God what you did to deserve this. It's not always something that you did or didn't do. I've found that to be true. When we are taught not to have sex before marriage, it's not done to punish us. It is done so that we are kept for our spouses. If you have sex before marriage and you have multiple partners, you enjoy what each one offers. When you finally get married, you now have the memory of all the things the other people did to you or with you and expect your spouse to do those same things. When they don't, you get bored and begin to wonder. Not having sex before marriage prevents these comparisons. You will only know this one person, and the sex will be everything you've always expected it to be.

Many spouses that have been cheated on live in silence and shame as if they did something wrong. I'm here to tell you that it's not your fault! You did nothing to deserve it. I know many people who know their spouse is cheating but are afraid to confront them for fear of losing them. They even fear what their family and friends are going to say. That was me. At the same time, the cheating spouse's friends and homies knew they are cheating. You feel like a fool and self-conscious when you are around them. Unfortunately, I can't give you advice on what to do in your situation. I was praying and crying out to God, "What should I do, and why is this happening to me?" I heard God say, "Are you going to walk, or are you going to stay and fight?" I had to stop crying, get myself together, and ask Him what He said. He clearly said again, "Are you going to walk, or are you going to stay and fight?" After thinking about it, I stayed and tried everything because I promised God I would. I took my vows seriously. There was an instance when a spouse in one situation took the word of the mistress over his wife's. That was the last straw. They didn't believe in divorce, but after doing all they could and praying to God about it, leaving with the children was the only way to keep their sanity and what little self-esteem they had left.

Infidelity affects not only the spouse but also the children. They can feel the tension in the home. You two are not speaking, the one being unfaithful is coming and going at all hours without a word or by lying about where they are going. If there is something that is not right in your relationship, talk about it with your spouse. They have no idea that you are unhappy or unsatisfied. Just keep in mind that if you want them to swing from the rafters because you use to date someone else who did, it doesn't mean that they will. They are two different people. You should also keep in mind that you married this person for who they are, and you shouldn't ask them to change who they are to make you happy in the area of sex. Love and appreciate them for who they are, just as they do you. Communication is the key. If your spouse doesn't want to do something, don't pressure them to do it or make them feel guilty because they don't. Mutual respect is key.

Be open to hearing what each other's desires are, but be respectful of each other's decisions—no judging or putting them down. You are *one*.

. . .

If we confess our sins, he is faithful and just and will forgive us our sins and purify us from all unrighteousness.

(1 John 1:9 NIV)

Dana's prayer:

God, I come to you asking for mercy for those who have committed infidelity. I pray that they would repent and ask for forgiveness. I pray that the lines of communication would be open in their marriage and that their spouse would be open to forgiving. I pray that your peace would reign in their home and that any children would not be affected. I also pray that any generational curses attached to the spirit of infidelity are broken in the name of Jesus. Thank you for freedom, Amen.

What are your takeaways?

____

____

____

____

____

____

____

How can you use this to move toward your destiny?

____

____

____

____

____

____

____

. . .

Your prayer:

____

____

____

____

____

____

____

CHAPTER TEN
J - JUST

behaving according to what is morally right, impartial, and fair.

Jesus was the greatest example to us for living a just life. He was morally right and fair. He was a shining example for us to look up to. There is no one greater! God sent him as an example in the flesh for us to model our lives after. Most of us search high and low for someone to lead us and guide us through our lives. Why? We have the perfect example and a Father like no other.

I have lived most of my life trying to live the way the Bible has instructed us to live, showing compassion and love and treating others the way I want to be treated. First Corinthians 11:1-2 (ESV) says, "Be imitators of me, as I am of Christ. Now I commend you because you remember me in everything and maintain the traditions even as I delivered them to you."

A great example of a just man was Dr. Martin Luther King Jr. He was truly a man after God's heart. He lived his life based on the principles by which Jesus lived. He was persecuted, hated, arrested, and killed. He was killed because the enemy knew that God had a plan for his life that would ultimately change the world. What the enemy didn't know was that God had already laid the foundation and elevated him to do exactly what he was supposed to do before he left this earth. In his own words, he was "a drum major for peace." He treated everyone the way he wished to be treated. He fought for those who didn't have a voice. He used his words, words given to him by God, and God's words written in the Bible, to get God's message across. He was open to helping everyone no matter what the cost to him. Micah 6:8 (NIV) says, "He has told you, O man, what is good; and what does the Lord require of you but to do justice, and to love kindness, and to walk humbly with your God?" He had a dream that justice would prevail in this world and that all people would be equal, because God made us all the same. He was so in tune with God his father, he prophesied his own death just as Jesus did when he had the last supper with the disciples. He was morally right, impartial, and fair.

Dr. King said, "It's right to be just and that you are willing to die for it." As long as you are doing what is right, you are never alone. God is always with you. God made it our nature to be just. The enemy has inserted people and things onto your path to throw you off course because he knows some of the plans God has for you. He only knows things in part just as we do. Only our Heavenly Father knows everything in whole. Striving to live a just life is rewarding and beneficial. Being just allows us to leave a life of peace. I'm not saying that life will be rosy each day, but that you will have God's peace that surpasses all understanding. You won't understand it, but you will expect it because it was promised to you. The Bible is a solid blueprint that shows us how we are to live a just life.

When it comes to marriage, being just is a foundational factor for a great marriage. When you take those vows to be true to one another, you've already entered a covenant with God and your spouse to keep yourself just for them—hence, morally right. You and your mate must be on the same page. Let's say that you don't drink, smoke, or have sex outside of your marriage, but you marry someone who doesn't share the same moral values as you. You begin to think that maybe you should lean toward doing some of the things your mate does to please him or make him happy. But at the same time, you feel yourself becoming unhappy. Are you willing to give up who you are and what you believe for this person and possibly be on a road to losing you? Marriage is all about compromise, but one thing it is not about is losing who God created you to be. You both should be on a journey together. Yes, the husband is the head of the wife, but God also gives us wisdom to know when the husband is not following our heavenly Father.

Strive daily to live a life that's impartial and fair. Always treat others the way you desire to be treated, and the blessings will come back to you in ways that you have never imagined!

You will experience all these blessings if you obey the Lord your God. (Deut. 28:2 NLT)

Dana's prayer:

Father, I come to you now as humbly as I can asking you to show me how to be just, how to live a life pleasing to you while not compromising who I am in the process. God, I ask that you guide my footsteps as I journey through each day. I pray that I am open to receiving all directions and instructions so that I might live a pleasing life as your son Jesus did. I give you all glory, honor, and praise. In Jesus's name, Amen.

What are your takeaways?

____

____

____

____

____

____

How can you use this to move toward your destiny?

____
____
____
____
____
____
____

Your prayer:

____
____
____
____
____
____
____

CHAPTER ELEVEN
K - KINDNESS

the quality of being friendly, generous, and
considerate

Remember that saying that you catch more flies with honey than with vinegar? That tells me that we can go further in our relationships with kindness than with anger. One thing I've been trying to do consistently is send my husband a word of encouragement and love each morning via text. One thing that I've learned is that he's come to look forward to it.

Kindness goes far beyond buying your spouse things. Kindness also includes listening to what your spouse has to say and why they are saying it, sitting together having meaningful conversations. Instead of always trying to be right, keep an open mind and remember your vows to love, honor, and cherish each other.

There are many times in relationships and marriages where we are not as kind to our partners and spouses as we are to strangers. We treat other people with more kindness and respect than the person we have vowed to love, honor, and cherish for the rest of our lives.

Ephesians 4:32 (NIV) says, "Be kind to one another, tenderhearted, forgiving one another, as God in Christ forgave you." It's clear that we are being instructed to do this with everyone, especially with our spouses and partners. When you have a disagreement or an argument with your spouse, many times you are upset and in your feelings. You can be so angry that you say or do things to your spouse that you would not normally. Yes, we are all human and this can happen, but those things can be totally out of character for us. There may be profanity, silence, physical abuse, or just saying things that totally shock your partner. On the other hand, we can have a confrontation with someone else and treat them with more kindness than we show our spouse.

I had an experience where I was being cheated on and knew it but never said anything. Even after there was proof of the infidelity, I stayed and continued as if nothing ever happened. I was showing kindness and sometimes thought I was showing too much kindness. (That's the human side of me.) The spiritual side of me was remembering my vows and what the Bible said about marriage and being a good wife. No one deserves to be treated as a floor mat, but we will always be treated as such if we continue to allow it. Everyone has a breaking point, and mine was having the mistress's word taken over mine (the wife).

First Thessalonians 5:11 (NIV) says, "Therefore encourage one another and build one another up, just as you are doing."

Dana's prayer:

Father, I come to you now asking that you give us direction on how to be kind to one another. God I know this seems like a simple thing to do, but we have shown that it is one of the most difficult things to do. I pray that our eyes (spiritual, and natural) are open to see the examples you put before us. I also pray that our ears are open to hear your instructions. I pray that we will focus on being kind to everyone so that it becomes a natural part of our being. I thank you in advance for this awesome gift you have given us. I praise you and bless your name, Amen.

53

What are your takeaways?

____

____

____

____

____

____

____

How can you use this to move toward your destiny?

____

____

____

____

____

____

____

Your prayer:

____

____

____

____

____

____

____

CHAPTER TWELVE
L - LOVE
an intense feeling of deep affection

Sometimes it's lonely when you're married. You live in the same house, but you still feel alone. There are days when all you want is a hug. No sex required. Just a touch from the one person you stood before God and vowed to be there with in good and bad, but you can't even get that.

I've often been told that love is an action word. Showing someone you love them is more important than saying it. Well, doesn't hugging or holding the hand of your spouse fit into that definition of what love is supposed to be? Because I love you, I desire to be near you and with you. When you love someone, you make sacrifices. We long for love, and we long to be loved. "Above all, keep loving one another earnestly, since love covers a multitude of sins" (1 Pet. 4:8 ESV).

The Bible tells us of many instances where people were willing to give up something or someone they loved more than anything on earth. One person was Abraham. Genesis 22:2-3 (ESV) says, "He said, 'Take your son, your only son Isaac, whom you love, and go to the land of Moriah, and offer him there as a burnt offering on one of the mountains of which I shall tell you.'" So Abraham rose early in the morning, saddled his donkey, and took two of his men with him, and his son Isaac. And he cut the wood for the burnt offering and arose and went to the place of which God had told him.

When Abraham had Isaac, he was one hundred years old. He believed God when he said he would have a child with his wife at their ages. On that mountain, Abraham was about to sacrifice Isaac, when an angel told him to stop. As he looked around, he saw the ram that God had sent for him to sacrifice instead of Isaac. Abraham was willing to sacrifice Isaac in order to obey God. He was willing to give up everything he'd been waiting for and the future he had planned because he had faith in God's promises.

The greatest example of unconditional love we have is found in John 3:16 (NIV), "For God so loved the world that he gave his one and only Son, that whoever believes in him shall not perish but have eternal life." Just imagine if your child gave his or her life to save you.

God has made many promises, but do we have the faith to believe what He's told us? God told me He would send the person He had just for me, but there were things I had to do to prepare myself to receive him. I had to let go of any lingering anger I had, I had to break generational and ancestral curses over my family so I would be free and not continue to fall into the same predicaments my ancestors found themselves in. I had to spend time with God to hear His instructions. He asked me what I wanted in a husband. I'd never thought about it. I just figured when mister right showed up, I would know. That was not the case. I had to prepare myself to receive my life partner mentally, emotionally, and spiritually. I found a composition book and began writing thetraits I desired my husband to have. You would be amazed at what you come up with when you allow the connection you have with God to guide you.

You must remain open to hear His voice, to let go of the past hurts, disappointments, and condemnations others have spoken over you. In order to receive love, you must first love yourself. If you don't love you, how can anyone else? My husband has helped me see myself the way he sees me. Because of my low self-esteem, it was hard for me to see myself the way he sees me. Mind you, I am older than he is, but he would tell me that I dressed as if I was much older than I was. A few of the women in the church told me the same thing when we went shopping together. They began picking clothes that I never would have thought about wearing. Because I didn't fully love myself, I wasn't able to see myself the way he and others saw me. He loves me unconditionally!

Above all, love each other deeply, because love covers over a multitude of sins.(1 Pet. 4:8 ESV)

Love is patient, love is kind. It does not envy, it does not boast, it is not proud. It does not dishonor others, it is not self-seeking, it is not easily angered, it keeps no record of wrongs. Love does not delight in evil but rejoices with the truth. It always protects, always trusts, always hopes, always perseveres. Love never fails. (1 Cor. 13:4-8 NIV)

Dana's prayer

Father God, I come to you now humbly asking for your forgiveness. Please forgive me for anything I have done or said that was not pleasing to you. God, I ask that your wisdom would fall upon your people, those desiring to find that love that only a husband or wife can give. I pray that they would begin to prepare themselves to receive that special gift remembering that they must first love themselves before they can receive love from someone else.

Father I also pray for those couples who are already married. I pray that the spark that once ignited their relationship begins to burn again. I know we sometimes come to a place where we become comfortable with each other and begin to take each other for granted without even knowing it. I ask that you open our eyes to see what is important and that we would hear your instructions on what we should do to bring the fire back. God, I thank you and bless your Holy name. Thank you for your love. In Jesus's name I pray, Amen.

What are your takeaways?

____
____
____
____
____
____
____

How can you use this to move toward your destiny?

____
____
____
____
____
____
____

Your prayer:

____
____
____
____
____
____

CHAPTER THIRTEEN

M - MARRIAGE

a joining, a man and a woman becoming one

Marriage was established by God in the garden of Eden with Adam and Eve. He put Adam to sleep and performed the first surgery on him. He removed one of his ribs and created Eve, who was supposed to be a helpmeet to Adam. God designed marriage so man would not be alone (Gen. 2:18). He intended for us to work together, to support one another, to complement one another, and to encourage one another. Marriage is a covenant, which is a pledge or promise of what you will do.

We have taken the sanctity of marriage and made it into something negative. It's become so negative that people don't even want to get married. We have shown marriage as a battle, a battle for control over the other spouse and maybe even the kids. We have shown that we are selfish and have a spirit of condemnation toward our spouse, always pointing out their flaws instead of lifting them up. Many of us have seen the bad marriages of our parents, and we learned that this is what marriage is, so we build on the same foundation our parents' marriage was built. We have to make a choice to break the curse or cycle. We have to want more. We have to desire what God intended marriage to be.

I am on my second marriage. When my first marriage began falling apart in front of me, all I could do was ask God what I had done to deserve what was happening to me and my marriage. I had an idea of what marriage was supposed to be. I thought I was supposed to cook, clean, iron, and support him in whatever he did. I didn't really have any thoughts of what I wanted or what I was supposed to receive. I still had little self-confidence and still kept my voice to myself. I never shared my feelings, thoughts, or ideas. I just went along with it all. The Bible says we are to be submissive, but I don't think he intended for me or you to be a punching bag physically or metaphorically. Ephesians 5:22-24 (ESV) says: "Wives, submit to your own husbands, as to the Lord. For the husband is the head of the wife even as Christ is the head of the church, his body, and is himself its Savior." No changes were made until I made a decision I couldn't do it any longer. I prayed that God would understand that I had given my all and that I had no more to give.

Marriage was designed to glorify God. It was for us to be an example of how Jesus supports and loves the church. We are to do the same thing. When we show our spouses our flaws and they choose to love us anyway, that is a prime example of what Jesus did for the church when the people were in the temple exchanging money and selling all kinds of things which went against what they were to do.

The marriage covenant is a commitment between a man and a woman, who have vowed before God and their families to remain together until they die. It's a lifetime commitment. Before you decide to get married, make sure that you are ready to be fully committed to this one person for the rest of your life. Are you comfortable vowing before God that you will be with this person for the rest of your life? That you will share the good and the bad? Are you committed to working through any situation that may come up that will test your faith, your fidelity, or your honesty?

. . .

Dana's prayer:

Father, I come to you giving you praise and blessings. I pray for those who are not married and have a desire to be. I pray that they would keep their hearts and spiritual ears open to hear your direction. You already have the person who's perfect for them. I pray that they will wait patiently, but in the process, stick close to God. Father, I pray for those who are already married. I pray that they would remember that they are not in it alone but that you are with them. All they have to do is to give their marriage to you. Help them remember that You are the author and the finisher of everything. I pray that they will rely on you for guidance when there is confusion, discourse, and doubt in the marriage. God, have your way in Jesus' name, Amen.

What are your takeaways?

____
____
____
____
____
____
____

How can you use this to move toward your destiny?

____
____
____
____
____
____

Your prayer:

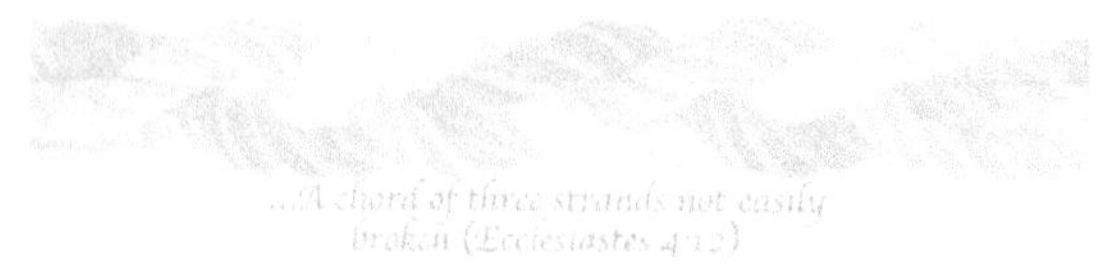

CHAPTER FOURTEEN
N - NOT NOW
when God says the time is not right

As kids, we played house. There was a mama, a daddy, and children. We didn't know it at the time, but we were preparing for marriage. We emulated what we saw at home and on TV. Marriage is something ordained and designed by God. If we are truly listening to His voice, then we can hear Him speak. He says, "Yes, that's the person for you," and then you hear His voice say, "No, not now." He's telling you that's the person I have sent you, but now is not the time for you to come together.

As we've matured, we've learned to pray and ask God for what we want, need, and desire. After all, Luke 11:9 (ESV) says, "And I tell you, ask, and it will be given to you; seek, and you will find; knock, and it will be opened to you." He wants to give us the desires of our heart, but only if it's going to help us. Sometimes, He allows things that aren't good for us because we keep asking, pursuing, and getting involved when it's not in our best interest. He will sit back and watch as we go through trying times because of our decision and wait for us to realize that He wanted the best for us. So that "not now" that you didn't listen to has turned into a whole mess that has you spinning out of control. God is our Father, and just like our earthly parents, He doesn't want to see us hurt, but He will allow us to do something that will hurt us if we insist.

John 11:1-45 tells us the story of Lazarus. Lazarus's sisters, Mary and Martha, sent Jesus a note when Lazarus became sick. Jesus was ministering someplace else and did not go right away. Jesus told the disciples that Lazarus was asleep. The disciples said it would be okay to wait. They didn't understand that Lazarus was dead. Jesus and his disciples went to the village where Lazarus lived. Jesus went to the tomb where he was buried, with Mary, Martha, and all those gathered at the house. Jesus prayed to God. After praying, he stood up and told Lazarus to rise. He walked out of the tomb wrapped in his burial cloth. They unwrapped him, and he went home. This was a prime example of God saying, "Not now." Yes, he died, but he had a greater purpose. It was to be an example that Jesus was indeed the son of God because only he could perform such a miracle.

Dana's prayer

Father, I bless your Holy name. I come to you praying that we would wait patiently until you determine the time is right for us to receive what you have for us. I pray that we would be open to receiving the spouse you have sent. I pray they would prepare themselves, too, for their forever mate. I bless your Holy name. Thank you, God. Amen.

What are your takeaways?

____

____

____

____

____

____

How can you use this to move toward your destiny?

Your prayer:

CHAPTER FIFTEEN
O - ONE

becoming one with your spouse means that
you put them and the marriage relationship
above all else, so honor your spouse and the
marriage; become one flesh.

"Then the man said, 'This at last is bone of my bones and flesh of my flesh; she shall be called Woman, because she was taken out of Man.' Therefore a man shall leave his father and his mother and hold fast to his wife, and they shall become one flesh" (Gen. 2:23-24 ESV).

God designed marriage to be the coming together of two people becoming one. This is what Adam was talking about in Genesis 2:24 when he said man is supposed to leave his father and mother to unite with his wife, and they become one flesh. God established marriage to be a lifelong commitment (Ecc. 9:9) where husbands and wives are supposed to love and respect each other (Eph. 5:28, 33). The Bible also tells us that husbands and wives are to be bonded together with similar beliefs, goals, and objectives (2 Cor. 6:14). Becoming one, we develop a close bond. We complement each other in so many ways. Companionship in marriage was built into us. In Proverbs 18:22 (NKJV), God says, "He who finds a wife finds a good thing and obtains favor from the Lord." Have you ever noticed how couples who have been together for many years know what the other is thinking because they finish each other's sentences? That is a perfect example of becoming one.

Becoming one requires commitment and dedication. Generations before us worked hard to keep their families and their marriages together. They fought through many obstacles and much opposition. Opposition from family and friends not supporting them, and obstacles such as financial hardships, infidelity, and the like.

Ecclesiastes 9:9 (KJV) says, "Live joyfully with the wife whom you love all the days of your life." Marriage vows contain the phrase "til death do us part." God intends for marriage to be a commitment for life. In marriage and relationships, there has to be love and respect. These are the foundations marriage is built upon. When you are alone, you have your own goals, visions, dreams, and desires, but when you marry and become one, God gives you new dreams, visions, and desires together. This doesn't mean that you give up your individuality. It simply means that He's given you a new corporate vision that will lead you together to your joint destiny.

Dana's prayer

God, you are worthy. I thank you for your love, your kindness, your peace, and your compassion. I come to you today asking that you would be with your children who have made a commitment to that special someone you have placed in their lives, the one they have decided to spend the rest of their lives with, the person they have become one with. Father, I pray that they would always remember the reason they chose each other, that they would build each other up and not tear each other down with their words. God, I pray against the spirit of division right now in Jesus's name. Satan, you have no authority over the marriages that God has joined together. I pray that the power and authority that rests in God would rule over their relationships. I also pray for those who desire to become one with the person you have set aside only for them. I pray that they would remain open and ready to receive the blessing. In Jesus's name, Amen.

What are your takeaways?

____
____
____
____
____
____

How can you use this to move toward your destiny?

____
____
____
____
____
____

Your prayer:

____
____
____
____
____
____

CHAPTER SIXTEEN

P - PRAYER

conversation with God

Prayer is the foundation of any relationship. Without it, we fail and fall. We look at prayer as something so difficult. It's this big thing that only certain people can do, and God will hear only them. The truth is, there is no right or wrong way to pray. Prayer is just a conversation with God. The Bible doesn't say that we have to come to God with big words or long, drawn-out speeches. The Bible gives a clear example of how to pray to God, but for some reason, we've forgotten that He put it in the book.

Matthew 6:9-1 (ESV) gives us the foundation for prayer, and it simply says: "This, then, is how you should pray: 'Our Father which art in heaven, Hallowed be thy name. Thy kingdom come, Thy will be done in earth, as it is in heaven. Give us this day our daily bread. And forgive us our debts, as we forgive our debtors. And lead us not into temptation, but deliver us from evil: For thine is the kingdom, and the power, and the glory, for ever. Amen.'"

Now let's break this down a little bit more so that there is no misunderstanding. You will no longer think prayer is too hard!

Verse 9: "Our Father which art in heaven." This is you speaking to God the Father saying, "Good morning, hello, what's up?"Verse

10: "Hallowed be thy name." *Hallowed* means "holy, exalted," so basically we are telling God that His name is holy and worthy of complete devotion.

Verse 11: "Thy kingdom come, Thy will be done in earth as it is in heaven." We can experience God's kingdom on earth, we are praying for His will to manifest on earth just as it is in heaven. As children of God, we have a right to everything He has because we are his heirs. He desires to give us things beyond what we can imagine or comprehend, but there is one thing we must do before He can give it to us. We must ask. Not ask from a place of greed or selfishness, but from a place of humbleness and sincerity. Also remember to ask not just for you, but for others as well.

Verse 12: "Give us this day our daily bread." This is asking God to give us what is necessary to sustain us, nothing more and nothing less.

Verse 13: "And forgive us our debts, as we forgive our debtors." We are asking God to forgive for the things we owe others. For example, say you asked a friend to borrow some money, and time has passed, but you never repaid what you owed. You don't mention it, and your friend doesn't mention it, but neither of you have forgotten it. Now on the flip side, you lent your friend some money and they have not given it back to you. You've asked for it because you really needed it, but they said they didn't have it. It's strange that we look at these two situations as being different when they are exactly the same. We are asking God to forgive us for not repaying what we owe our friend and also remembering to forgive that friend who owes us.

"And lead us not into temptation." God would never lead us into situations where we are tempted. We are asking Him to direct us around things, people, and circumstances that could lead us down a path that is not pleasing to Him.

"But deliver us from evil." We are asking God to keep us away from anything that might tempt us and keep us out of God's will.

"For thine is the kingdom, and the power, and the glory, for ever." There is a key to your prayer being effective. Do you know what that is? It's you accepting Him (God) into your heart as your personal savior. In case you didn't know, God sent His Son Jesus down to earth to show us how we are to live. His plan was never for Jesus to stay with us, but to teach us and show us the way by being a living example. After his time with us was up and his job was finished, God made the ultimate sacrifice by having His Son die on the cross for our sins.

The Bible gives us clear instructions on how we should accept Him. And guess what? It's simple (Matt.10:9-11).

I believe that all relationships should include prayer. Prayer as an individual between you and God, prayer together as husband and wife, and prayer together when you take the step of becoming engaged. Prayer is the foundation for any relationship. It's the foundation of your relationship with God and the relationship between you as a couple and God. He already knows the desires of your heart; He just wants to hear it from you.

Before you say, "I do," one of the things you should discuss is spending time together with God as a couple. If your fiancé doesn't agree or has a problem with it, ask why. If the reason doesn't sit well with you, perhaps you need to take time to see if they are the right person for you. You see, God won't send you someone who will take you away from Him. He will send you someone who brings you closer.

Sometimes prayer seems like a big sacrifice. We always seem to have excuses about why we can't do it. I had to work late and I'm so tired, I'm going to bed. I'll pray in the morning. Guess what, that morning rarely comes. How about this one: "My kids have so many activities. When I get home I have to cook dinner and get them ready for the next day after helping them with their homework. I'll spend a few minutes in prayer as soon as I get them in bed." Well, the phone rings after you get the kids settled, and you forget about prayer because the conversation with the person on the phone becomes more important than the conversation you said you would have with God.

The Bible tells us that God is a jealous God and you should put nothing and no one before Him (Exod. 34:14). All the excuses we make in our daily lives about why we can't spend that quality time with our Father, are kind of idols. We make time for anything and everything else we want to do and have to do, but God gets the short end of the stick. I am guilty of this as well. I'm speaking from experience. Just like you make a schedule of the family's daily activities, add a block and call it "Time with My Father." You don't have to go straight in for an hour. Start small. Try fifteen minutes a day and make it the same time each day. Just as a baby learns to walk, we must learn to make a sacrifice of our time. God has already given us so much. All He wants is for you to spend time with Him.

Rejoice always, pray without ceasing, give thanks in all circumstances; for this is the will of God in Christ Jesus for you. (1 Thess. 5:16-18 NIV)

Dana's prayer;

Father, I come to you now thanking you for sending Jesus to bear all my sins on the cross, for enduring my pain. God, I ask that you be patient with me as I learn to make changes in my life to spend quality time with you. This isn't going to be easy for me because I have so many distractions in my life. I will make an appointment with you on my calendar daily. I will not only come to you with the things that are going wrong and tell you about all the people who did me wrong that day, but I will also spend time thanking you for all the things you are in my life. You are my provider, my strong tower, my shield and protector, my deliverer, my light in the darkness, and my friend. I thank you for being there for me when no one else is. God, I ask that you keep my mind focused on this promise, this commitment. I thank you in advance for the awesome time I will have when I spend time talking to you every day. In Jesus's name, Amen.

What are your takeaways?

____
____
____
____
____
____
____

How can you use this to move toward your destiny?

____
____
____
____
____
____
____

Your prayer:

____
____
____
____
____
____
____

CHAPTER SEVENTEEN
Q - QUIET SPIRIT
being obedient to God and His Word

If you heard someone say you have a quiet spirit, would you be offended? Many of us take that negatively when it's actually a compliment. Right now I'm talking to the women, but, men, please don't go to the next chapter, because there are some nuggets in here for you too.

Many relationships start out great. We are excited to spend time together, we hang on each other's every word, and we do whatever we can to make sure the other person is happy. Oftentimes after being married for a while, we get comfortable and take each other for granted, the kids come, and things begin to go downhill from there. Our words can become harsh and unkind, or nonexistent.

Having a quiet sprit is all about being obedient to God and His Word. Many women tear their husbands down and break their spirits by the things they say and do. That is one reason husbands may stray. The Bible instructs us to build our husbands up (Prov. 31:12 ESV).

We are to respect our husbands. Support his ideas and help him achieve them in any way you can. Give him praise. Don't always concentrate on his negative; focus on the positive. It is not your job to convict him; leave that up to God. Both of you should willingly show intimacy toward each other. Communicate your wants, needs, and desires. Remember, sex is one of the main areas the enemy uses to destroy marriages. Don't leave the door open.

Don't try to take over. Many times as women we have had to do just about everything ourselves, which causes us just to jump in and do what needs to be done. Well, when you get married, you have to learn to let go of some of those things and allow your husband to do what he needs to do. When I remarried, I didn't realize I was doing things that he should have been doing until he said something. We are there to be a helpmeet. Remember, you are no longer in it alone. Allow him to lift you up instead of you always lifting everyone else up.

Ask your husband for his advice. I try to ask if he likes an outfit I am looking at purchasing. Many times he likes it and I'm not too sure about it. That's because I'm used to being conservative. I've always been self-conscious about my body, but I try to remember that if he likes it and it doesn't reveal too much, I can live with it. You see, it's the little things that bring you together. Also remember a husband not only wants a wife that looks good on the outside, but on the inside as well. Be a woman after God's own heart (1 Sam. 13:14).

"Favor is deceitful, and beauty is vain: but a woman that feareth the Lord, she shall be praised. Give her of the fruit of her hands; and let her own works praise her in the gates" (Prov. 31:30-31 KJV). Ladies, did you know that when you are praised, recognized for doing a good job at work, or just complimented on your great attitude, your husband is happy just as if he received the praise. If you look close enough, his chest will probably be sticking out. It brings him joy to see someone else recognize the greatness he already knew was within you.

Don't stop being you. Just relax and let go of some things. Trust the man that you believe God sent to you. There is still plenty for you to do, but more than anything, there is peace in the house.

. . .

But let your adorning be the hidden person of the heart with the imperishable beauty of a gentle and quiet spirit, which in God's sight is very precious. (1 Pet. 3:4 ESV)

Dana's prayer:

Father, I come to you right now on behalf of all those women who have been holding on to the thinking that they are all alone in this world with no one to help them, but they have a husband right there ready, willing, and able. I pray in the matchless name of Jesus that you would break that spirit off of them. Remove the scales from their eyes and let them see that they don't have to do it alone. God, I also pray for the husbands right now and ask that they would see that their wife is not trying to take anything away from them, but she's done everything alone for so long she doesn't know how to let go and let you. I pray for open hearts, open minds, and a loving spirit. I also pray that the words they speak to each other are words that will build up and not tear down. That they would allow you to lead and guide them in everything they do and that decisions are made together. What God has joined, let no man separate. I thank you in advance for the manifestation of this prayer. I give you praise, Amen.

What are your takeaways?

____

____

____

____

____

____

. . .

How can you use this to move toward your destiny?

____

____

____

____

____

____

____

Your prayer:

____

____

____

____

____

____

____

CHAPTER EIGHTEEN
R - RESPONSIBILITY

having a duty to deal with something or
having control over someone

Well, gentlemen, this is for you. Ladies, don't go anywhere. There are some takeaways here for you too. There are some things husbands and those desiring to have a wife someday have a responsibility to do for their wives.

The first and most important thing is to love and protect her (Eph. 5:25-29). You should honor her publicly and in private. You should also protect her reputation. One way to do that is not to speak about her badly when you get around your friends (1 Pet. 3:7). Always show her respect.

Husbands are also instructed to provide spiritual leadership to her and the family (Eph. 6:4). Let's say your wife has more biblical knowledge than you do and spends time in prayer and worship. It's still your responsibility to show leadership. Never compare your spirituality to each other's. God made each of you differently and has given you exactly what He wanted you to have. Never think what is inside you is not enough. It's more than enough! Set up a time to study together. Read scriptures and talk about what you think about what you read. Most important, lead her in prayer. You will build a closer connection when you worship God together.

Spend time with your wife and enjoy each other. Designate a day or night for dates, just the two of you. You could go out to dinner, stay home and have movie night, or even have a picnic in the house in the middle of the living room. The only thing that matters is that you are together enjoying each other's company and sharing things that are on your hearts (Prov. 18:22).

Husbands, love your wives, as Christ loved the church and gave himself up for her. (Eph. 5:25 ESV)

Dana's prayer:

God, I come to you now honoring you for your grace and mercy. I pray right now for all the husbands and those who desire to be husbands. I pray that they will stay close to you so they can learn exactly what it means to be a Christian husband, to learn what their responsibilities are. I pray that they would be open to hearing your instructions and committed to carrying them out. I pray that their eyes, hearts, and minds are open. I pray that their wives would see you moving and guiding them and that they would move as you have instructed them. Follow him as he follows you. I pray that their relationships would glorify you and be a light in the earth to other couples. That they would be a shining example of exactly what you intend marriage to be. I pray that you would bless them, protect them, strengthen them, and nurture them in Jesus's name, Amen.

What are your takeaways?

____

____

____

____

____

____

____

How can you use this to move toward your destiny?

____

____

____

____

____

____

____

Your prayer:

____

____

____

____

____

____

____

CHAPTER NINETEEN
S - SACRIFICE

surrendering a possession as a offering to
God giving up the lesser important for the
most important

When we make sacrifices in relationships and marriage, they are usually to make the other person better in some way. Ladies, have you ever found yourself fixing plates for dinner and giving your husband the bigger piece of meat? That was a sacrifice: giving up something you wanted to make your partner happy.

Another example of sacrifice is supporting your spouse or partner when they want to make a life change, like starting their own business. The spouse who wants to start the business has the concept and the means to make it happen, but they don't know anything about the things needed before opening it. The other partner handles the marketing, registering the business with the state, website design, and more. Together you work as a team. Sacrifices must be made to accomplish goals in relationships to prepare for the future. Sacrifice is an action, not just words. It's when one person freely chooses to give up something without resentment. We can look at sacrifice as a mustard seed.

He said to them, "Because of your little faith. For truly, I say to you, if you have faith like a grain of mustard seed, you will say to this mountain, 'Move from here to there,' and it will move, and nothing will be impossible for you" (Matt. 7:20 ESV). It's actually the little things that mean the most.

Dana's prayer:

Father, I bless your Holy name. You are truly worthy of all praise. I thank you for this day, a day of new beginnings. God, I pray that those who read this will understand what sacrificing is all about. That it's not about giving in or giving up, but about giving unselfishly and receiving things that they never imagined possible. Father, I pray that hardened hearts will be softened, that past hurts will not hinder the one reading this from receiving all you have for them and that they will be open to receiving all the blessings you have mapped out for them. I pray all these things in the matchless name of Jesus, Amen.

What are your takeaways?

____

____

____

____

____

____

____

How can you use this to move toward your destiny?

____

____

____

____

Your prayer:

CHAPTER NINE
T - TEMPTATION

the desire to do something, especially
something wrong or unwise

No temptation has overtaken you that is not common to man. God is faithful, and he will not let you be tempted beyond your ability, but with the temptation he will also provide the way of escape, that you may be able to endure it (1 Cor. 10:13).

Temptation is a part of our daily lives, but it's so subtle, sometimes we don't notice it. For instance, you're on a journey to better health and you've decided not to eat sweets. You go out to get lunch, and you walk by your favorite bakery. The smells that are coming from inside are incredible. The delicious items in the window begin speaking to you. They're saying, "Come in. One won't hurt you. You can work it off later."

That is just one example of temptation. The Bible tells us that Jesus was tempted by Satan before his crucifixion (Luke 4:1-13). In Luke 4:3 (NIV), Satan said, "If you are the Son of God, tell this stone to become bread." Jesus's response in Luke 4:4 (NIV) was, "It is written: 'Man shall not live on bread alone.'" He understood that if Jesus went through with it, he would be short. Jesus's sacrifice was paramount to our freedom from Satan. Had Jesus not gone through with it, our world would be in even greater chaos than it's in now. When it comes to marriage and relationships, there are always temptations. You see, what I've learned is that when God has something great in store for you and/or your spouse, the enemy will try to distract you and shift your focus to something or someone you would not usually entertain.

I've been working on this book for almost a year. It should have been done at least six months ago, but there were many distractions, trials, and things that I believe were supposed to be temptations. When I look back at times in my life where I was on a path I felt was ordained by God, the enemy sent men as a distraction or temptation. I'm not sure if it's because he thought I would be easily distracted and tempted because of the things I experienced as a child, the molestation and my promiscuous nature possibly making it easy for me to be tempted by men. Have you ever noticed that when you are in a relationship, men or women come from nowhere trying to get your attention, but when you are not in a relationship, they are nowhere to be found? I think that's pretty funny. Hence my thoughts surrounding temptation.

Job was tempted by Satan. In fact, God allowed it. In Job 1:6-22, we find out that the Lord asked Satan if he had considered his servant Job. He was a blameless, upstanding man who feared God and turned from evil. Satan said, "Wait a minute, isn't he the one you have a hedge of protection around? Protection around his home, property, and everything he owns?" The Lord said, "Yes." The Lord also told Satan that he could tempt Job but that he couldn't touch him. So Satan took his family, his property, and everything he had. Job never cursed God. He continued to praise Him and reverence Him. This shows us that God allows us to be tempted. Let's look at temptation as a test.

When those men and women come from nowhere trying to get your attention and draw you away from the person you are in a relationship with, look at it as a test. Are you devoted and focused on that relationship enough to say, "No I'm not interested.

I'm married (or engaged)"? There have been times before I was married where men would approach me, but I could already tell what they wanted. It was a test, to see if I would remain faithful to God and focused on the path He had me on at that particular time. So temptation can also be considered a test. Do we look at these situations as temptations, or are we just so flattered or feeling like we are not getting the attention we need, want, and deserve from our mates that we don't even think about it? I will not let the temptation of attention keep me from *all* God has for me!

Another major temptation we deal with is food. Many Americans battle the bulge daily. I just realized that I am an emotional eater. I don't celebrate with food; I find myself doing more comfort eating when under stress or pressure. Have you ever decided to lose weight and make better food choices, and the day you start, everything looks amazing? Even foods that never would have interested you. The temptation of food is a major distraction to keep you from your destiny. It can cause physical problems like high blood pressure, diabetes, heart attacks, and many other issues. It can also lead to mental health problems such as depression. You may have a feeling of low self-esteem and you feel like food is all you have, the only thing you can count on. Food doesn't judge me. I had to realize that in order for me to be the best me I can be and move into the destiny God has designed for me, I have to take control of the power I give to food. I will not let the temptation of food keep me from *all* that God has for me!

You have the power over any temptation that comes your way. Just remember that it is a test leading you to your destiny or a distraction to keep you from your destiny. Remember Job; he was tested to see how strong his faith and love for God were.

No temptation has overtaken you that is not common to man. God is faithful, and he will not let you be tempted beyond your ability, but with the temptation he will also provide the way of escape, that you may be able to endure it.

(1 Cor. 10:13 ESV)

Dana's prayer:

Father, I come to you now thanking you for your guidance, direction, and spirit of discernment. I pray that my eyes are open to see temptation when it comes my way and that I will be able to know if it's a test or a distraction to keep me from all you have for me. Thank you for the journey that is ahead of me. In Jesus's name, Amen.

What are your takeaways?

____

____

____

____

____

____

____

How can you use this to move toward your destiny?

____

____

____

____

____

____

____

. . .

Your prayer:

CHAPTER TWENTY-ONE
U - UNFORGIVENESS

a grudge against someone who has offended
you

Holding on to unforgiveness can lead to so many negative things for you physically, mentally, and spiritually. Unforgiveness can poison your relationships and marriage. Holding on to it can destroy your relationship if you don't try to heal and confront those things that are at the root of the situation.

First Peter 5:8 (AMP) says, "Be sober [well balanced and self-disciplined], be alert and cautious at all times. That enemy of yours, the devil, prowls around like a roaring lion [fiercely hungry], seeking someone to devour." Holding on to unforgiveness opens the door to the enemy. I've been in situations where I have been hurt, and the hurt caused me to become angry, and the anger led to resentment and bitterness. All these things added together equal unforgiveness. I've found myself holding on to all these feelings, and as a result, I've been physically in pain and mentally distracted and conflicted.

God extends forgiveness to us every day, but we don't offer it to others. In Matthew 18:21-35, we learn about a king who had a servant who owed him a huge debt that the king knew he wouldn't be able to pay back, so the king forgave him. Now that same servant who was forgiven by the king had lent his friend some money. The friend wasn't able to pay it back. Do you know what the man did to the friend? He had him thrown in jail. The king had forgiven him, but he wasn't willing to forgive his friend for the same offense.

I remember a time in my life when it seemed as if everything was going my way. I had purchased a house and had gone back to college. All of a sudden things got weird. I received a phone call one day from a car dealer telling me my husband, who we will call Monty (to protect the guilty person's identity), applied for a loan, and they needed to verify my information for a car loan. My response was, "Excuse me?" He repeated himself, and after I closed my mouth from disbelief, I told him that he was not my husband. I then received a letter saying my credit card account was closed and that I had to pay it or they were going to send me to collections. I didn't have a credit card. I had also cosigned for someone who defaulted on the bill, and I had to pay that. It seemed as if anything that had to do with money and my credit was out of control. I didn't have a car at the time, so I had to take trains and several busses to get to the company in the middle of nowhere to look at the credit application someone had filled out in my name. I knew immediately who had forged my name.

Well, in the process of trying to pay my regular bills and the defaulted bill, my bills fell behind. At the time, I was more concerned about the defaulted bill. Never having that happen to me before, I was terrified of not paying it off. In the process, my mortgage payments fell behind. I started getting letters from my mortgage company threatening to take my house I had worked so hard to get. After a while there was no way for me to dig myself out of the hole I was in. I got the foreclosure letter and was depleted, angry, and all alone. Now what was I going to do, and where were my son and I going to go? I didn't tell anyone what was going on. How was I going to tell my child that we had to leave our home without telling him why? I was so ashamed and embarrassed.

For many years I had unforgiveness in my heart toward those

two individuals for what they had done and tried to do, but what I've learned since then is that God takes us through experiences to see what we are going to do. Are we going to make moves to get out of the situation we are in, or are we going to stay stuck in the pity party we're having? I was sick for a long time, and now I believe it was partly due to unforgiveness. I had to make a conscious decision to forgive them so I could be free.

Unforgiveness is like a scab you keep pulling, but when it tries to heal, you pull it off again. You are in the process of continually causing pain by pulling it off again and again. After you pray to God for help with your unforgiveness, you have to let it go. I forgave one of them, but I really believe that I put the other unforgiveness in a box and put it on the shelf, not intending to pick it up again. Because it's on the shelf, I can pick it up at any time and relive the bitterness, disbelief, hurt, anger, pain, and betrayal caused. I realized I had not fully let the unforgiveness go. When a situation occurs with Monty, I'm reminded that he hasn't changed, and I get mad all over again. While writing this book, I came to a point where I forgave Monty for what he did to me, and I pray that God will give me strength when I see him continuing to do things to other people. I've found myself trying to comfort and calm other people down when Monty starts his shenanigans again.

God's desire is for us to be free. He did not intend for us to live in a state that causes us pain physically and mentally. That prevents us from getting closer to Him. We aren't able to focus on God when we are holding unforgiveness in our hearts. We can't give him our all when we're holding unforgiveness in our hearts. He will help us release the unforgiveness. All we have to do is acknowledge that we have it, that we don't want to carry it any longer, and that we desire to be free!

. . .

Bearing with one another and, if one has a complaint against another, forgiving each other; as the Lord has forgiven you, so you also must forgive. (Col. 3:13 ESV)

Dana's prayer

Father, I come to you now in the matchless name of Jesus giving you all the glory, all the honor, and all the praise. Father, I thank you for being patient with me as I've made a decision to release the unforgiveness I've been holding on to. Father, I ask you to forgive me for holding Monty captive all these years. I pray that he would see his errors and repent. I thank you, God, for never giving up on me. I thank you for freedom, and I thank you that the spirit of heaviness will no longer weigh me down. I thank you for my healing mentally, physically, and spiritually. Thank you, Jesus, for new beginnings. In Jesus's name, Amen.

What are your takeaways?

____

____

____

____

____

____

____

How can you use this to move toward your destiny?

____

____

____

____

____

Your prayer:

CHAPTER TWENTY-TWO
V - VISION

to think or plan the future with imagination or wisdom

"The Lord answered me: 'Write the vision; make it plain on tablets, so he may run who reads it. For still the vision awaits its appointed time: it hastens to the end—it will not lie. If it seems slow, wait for it; it will surely come; it will not delay'" (Hab. 2:2-3 ESV).

As my coach and mentor Lenika Scott says, "You have to see it before you see it." Before getting married, couples should come together for a discussion about their vision. If you've decided to attend premarital counseling, you may discuss this as part of it. There is not only a vision for you individually, but there is also a combined vision. This vision could include your vision for finances, work, home, and play. It is crucial that you are both on the same page. If you have different goals, dreams, and objectives, your journey together will be rocky. If you don't agree on money, how to raise the kids, or even where to eat, how can you combine your visions? The Bible says two people cannot walk together unless they agree. Marriages don't stand a chance if the couple is divided.

Many people lose sight of their individual vision when they get married. It could be because their spouse doesn't support it and speaks negatively about it, and they are discouraged and no longer interested in pursuing it. It is so important that you don't lose sight of your vision. You may have to pray and ask God to guide you and help you stay focused on it. Your vision gives you a clear sense of purpose. Also keep in mind that as you grow, your vision grows and changes. The plan He gave you at twenty may not be the same as the one He has for you when you are forty.

Wow. Planning a future with imagination and wisdom is an awesome thing. God has already given us the blueprints. He's mapped it all out for us. All we have to do is open our eyes in the spirit to be able to see it. Our futures are amazing. The businesses, inventions, and innovations that are assigned to us will blow our minds.

For the vision [is] yet for an appointed time, but at the end it shall speak, and not lie: though it tarry, wait for it; because it will surely come, it will not tarry. (Hab. 2:3 KJV)

Dana's prayer:

Father, I come to you giving you all glory, honor, and praise for who you are and what you've done. You are amazing, and I love you. I pray right now in the matchless name of Jesus that eyes will be opened to see and ears will be opened to hear the vision you have in store for your people. I pray that they will act with urgency and a sense of purpose. The window you open for us is only open for a specific period of time. God, I pray that we do not miss it. I thank you for trusting me with the blueprints for your people. I will walk with a sense of purpose, urgency, faith, and compassion. I pray your blessings overtake all of your people, especially those who think they do not have a vision. I thank you for having a plan for all of your children. Thank you for new beginnings. In Jesus's name, Amen.

· · ·

What are your takeaways?

____

____

____

____

____

____

How can you use this to move toward your destiny?

____

____

____

____

____

____

Your prayer:

____

____

____

____

____

____

CHAPTER TWENTY-THREE
W - WIFE

"He who finds a wife finds a good thing and
obtains favor from the Lord" (Prov. 18:22
ESV).

A Christian wife is a woman who honors God and obeys His word. She also maintains a godly relationship with her husband and others in her life. A godly wife focuses on God and His instructions. No matter what it looks like, no matter what sacrifices need to be made, she does it with passion and diligence knowing that her trials and experiences are not in vain.

Women were created to be helpmeets. When God created Eve, He intended her and Adam to reign over the earth together as equals. In Hebrew, the word Ezer means "warrior," and the word Kenegdo means "opposite as to him." This means that women are co-warriors with men and that they are no greater or less than men. Eve was not an afterthought. She was presented to Adam in God's divine time. God said in Genesis 2:18 (KJV), "It is not good that man should be alone; I will make him an help meet for him."

Before I got married, I had a preconceived notion of what marriage was supposed to be. I thought it would be days full of sunshine, togetherness, cuddling, talking, meals together, honesty, faithfulness, and respect. I was in for a rude awakening. I thought my job in the relationship was to cook, clean, and take care of my family.

Many women today feel as if they are expected to be inferior to men and are supposed to take a back seat because the Bible talks about being submissive to your husband. Many men take that out of context and use it in a negative way and as a form of control over them. Ephesians 5:14-25 (KJV) says, "Now as the church submits to Christ, so also wives should submit to their husbands in everything. Husbands, love your wives, just as Christ loved the church and gave himself up for her." Not once did Christ treat the church in a negative way. He uplifted her, nurtured her, and taught her his ways and the ways of his father.

Proverbs 31 outlines the virtues of a good wife. A virtuous wife has high standards and morals. She focuses on being the right wife first then trusts God to give her a husband at the right time. She puts God first, and everything else will fall into place (Prov. 31:10-12, 26-27, Titus 2:3-4).

Give your husband loving submission. Ephesians 5 talks about someone who is filled with the spirit, with a melodious heart, singing, and making melody to the Lord (5:19). It says to thank God for what He's done for you (5:20), be submissive to one another in the fear of Christ (5:21), and follow his leadership (5:23). There is an exception: if your husband expects you to do something sinful, you can say no. God doesn't want you to compromise yourself for sin to satisfy your husband. He is supposed to lead you to God, not to the enemy. If he is asking you to dress provocatively, you shouldn't do it. It can entice other men. He is out of the will of God. Be discreet and chaste (Titus 2:5). If you are not for sale, watch what you wear. God has a higher authority than he does. Never let him physically abuse you (Col. 3:18). "In the same way, you wives be submissive to your own husbands so that even if any of them are disobedient to the word, they may be won without a word by the behavior of the wives" (1 Pet. 3:1 AMP). Don't tell your husband what to do. Ask him. You catch more flies with honey than with vinegar. Christ purified the church, so should husbands do for their wives.

In terms of physical romance, "For the reason a man shall leave his father and mother and shall be joined to his wife, and the two shall become one flesh" (Eph. 5:31 NIV). You are not to deprive your spouse of sex unless you are in a time of spiritual consecration. "The husband should fulfill his wife's sexual needs, and the wife should fulfill her husband's needs. The wife gives authority over her body to her husband, and the husband gives authority over his body to his wife. Do not deprive each other of sexual relations, unless you both agree to refrain from sexual intimacy for a limited time so you can give yourselves more completely to prayer. Afterward, you should come together again so Satan won't be able to tempt you because of your lack of self-control" (1 Cor. 7:3-5 NLT). Meet your husband's need for genuine respect. "Nevertheless, each individual among you also is to love his own wife even as himself, and the wife must see to it that she respects her husband" (Eph. 5:33 NASB). "In the same way, you wives, be submissive to your own husbands so that even if any of them are disobedient to the word, they may be won without a word by the behavior of their wives, as they observe your chaste and respectful behavior" (1 Pet. 3:1 NASB 1995). This doesn't mean that you are inferior to him.

Allow your husband to lead as long as he is allowing God to lead him. Don't correct him, don't tell him how to discipline the kids. Spend time with him. If you don't like the same movies or even sports, still sit with him. He needs encouragement from you. Thank him for providing for you and the family. Give him financial responsibility, avoid debt, establish a budget, live within your means, and be financially prudent and thrifty.

"These older women must train the younger women to love their husbands and their children. To live wisely and be pure, to work in their homes, to do good, and to be submissive to their husbands. Then they will not bring shame on the word of God" (Titus 2:4-5 NLT). Make your home a priority. My slogan for my personal chef business is "Bringing Families Back to the Table." We have stopped eating together. There was a time when families came together every day no matter where you were or what you were doing, to eat dinner together. "How blessed is everyone who fears the Lord, Who walks in His ways. When you shall eat of the fruit of your hands, You will be happy and it will be well with you. Your wife shall be like a fruitful vine within your house, your children like olive plants around your table. Behold, for thus shall the man be blessed Who fears the Lord" (Ps. 128:1-2 NASB 1995).

Do not be disrespectful to your husband. It's not always what you say; it's also about how you say it. Say what's on your mind, but don't put him down, especially in front of other people or even in front of your children (Prov. 31:26).

You will never be able to change your spouse. Ask God to fix you. Satan tries to send thoughts to discourage you in your marriage. Think about what you're going to say before you say it. You must have self-control (Prov. 15:1-2).

Dana's prayer

God, I thank you for a new day. I thank you for your love, your guidance, and your protection. Father, I thank you for being my provider, my friend, and my strong tower. You are awesome, magnificent, mighty, merciful, faithful, and majestic. I come to you thanking you for my husband. I thank you for hearing and answering my prayers. I ask now in Jesus's name that you will continue to teach me to be a better wife. To open not only my physical ears, eyes, and heart, but also those things in the spirit so that I might get my direction directly from you. I pray that I would be more attentive, supportive, and understanding. I ask that you show me what I need to work on in me and continue to remind me that I cannot change him, but that I can only change me. Thank you in Jesus's name, Amen.

. . .

What are your takeaways?

____

____

____

____

____

____

____

How can you use this to move toward your destiny?

____

____

____

____

____

____

____

Your prayer:

____

____

____

____

____

____

____

CHAPTER TWENTY-FOUR

Y - YEARN

have an intense feeling of longing for
something, typically something that one has
lost or been separated from

"**A**sk and it wit will be given to you; seek and you will find; knock and the door will be opened to you" (Matt. 7:7 NIV).

Growing up, I remember playing house. Someone was the mother, someone was the father, and someone played the children. We all had a yearning to be married and in a relationship. We didn't fully understand. I believe God put this desire in our DNA. After all, he created Eve so that Adam wouldn't be alone.

When I was in high school, I can't say that I really dated. On a few rare occasions my father allowed me to go out with a gentleman caller. My father was protective, and I didn't get to go out much. I started seeing the person I would later marry. We talked about getting married. I think I was more serious about it than he was. I was committed and already planning my wedding. I yearned to be married, to spend the rest of my life with the person I loved more than anything. Psalm 37:4 (ESV) says, "Delight yourself in the Lord, and he will give you the desires of your heart." Many times we don't spend time with God and share our heart when we are yearning for things, even our spouses, so how can He possibly give us the desires of our heart? I never talked to God to see if what I wanted lined up with what He wanted for my life.

I went to college away from home and away from the man I thought I'd marry. When Thomas Edison came up with the quote, "Absence makes the heart grow fonder," I think he had me in mind. My every thought was about him and what he was doing. I'd call him more than he called me, and when we did talk, the conversation was short and usually involved us listening to each other breathe. I felt that my heart was all in but his wasn't. It seemed as if he didn't have the same yearning for me that I had for him. We married, and we were finally together. I was excited and so happy. As time went on in a new state far away from my family and friends, I felt the loneliest I'd ever felt in my life with the person I had yearned to be with for so long. Our marriage didn't last very long, so I was alone again.

I spent many years of learning to be alone and talking to God about what happened in my marriage and what I needed to do to make sure it didn't happen in my next one. God told me to make a list of all the things I desired in a mate. I shared with him the desires of my heart, and he, in turn, gave me instructions. Mark 11:24 (ESV) says, "Therefore I tell you, whatever you ask in prayer, believe that you have received it, and it will be yours." Prayer allows you to see many options and to hear God speaking clearly. As I began writing the desires of my heart for my spouse, I was closing the journal one night and thought of another thing I wanted to add to my list. After I added it, I wrote at the top of the page, "God, please allow me to continue to add to this list as things come to my mind."

As I was moving through my life and not looking for anyone, God put the person who would become my husband right in front of me, and I didn't know it. Ladies, you are to be pursued and not to pursue. The funny thing is that He was praying to God for a wife, and each time he prayed, he said he saw my face. While playing basketball one day, he tore his Achilles and needed surgery. After surgery, he was determined to stay at his house and not with his parents. After his surgery, I decided to make sure he had food to eat while recuperating since he couldn't walk. When I went to his house, we stayed up for hours talking. It had been a long time since I had opened up to someone.

My son was planning a surprise engagement party for his soon-to-be wife. My co-pastor asked me if someone from our church could attend. He was also a friend of my son, so I said sure. Little did I know that it was a setup. While I was downstairs waiting for my son to get there, I didn't know that my girlfriend's husband was upstairs helping our guest get dressed. He gave him a suit and shoes so he could join the festivities. After the dinner was over, I was going to my car and he pulled up and gave me roses and candy. He said, "Happy birthday." It was Valentine's Day, and my birthday was the next day. I was surprised by the gesture and said thank you. I didn't expect it. I found out later that everyone in the house was working in the background trying to get us together. I was a deer in headlights, focused on what was in front of me.

I said all this to say that when God has a plan for your life, you may not see it at first, but know that He will reveal it when it's time. That surprise guest is now my husband. The traits and characteristics I had written on the list of things I wanted in a husband, I began seeing in him. Genesis 2:18 (ESV) says: "Then the Lord God said, 'It is not good that the man should be alone; I will make him a helper fit for him.'" I believe our relationship started with a yearning for something we hadn't found in our previous relationships. The Bible also says, "You have not because you ask not" (James 4:2 KJV). Ultimately, when you are yearning for something, write it down, pray without ceasing, and believe that God hears you and will respond.

Write the vision; make it plain on tablets, so he may run who reads it. (Hab. 2:2 ESV)

· · ·

Dana's prayer:

Father, I come to you now giving you all glory, honor, and praise. I pray right now that all who are reading this with a yearning inside would recognize it and be open to allowing it to manifest, remembering that God placed it there and that it is a part of their destiny. I pray in Jesus's name that they find that thing that was lost if it is your will for them. I pray that they are open and ready to receive that thing they are yearning for that may be right in front of them. I thank you and praise you for the wholeness it will add to their lives in Jesus's name, Amen.

What are your takeaways?

____

____

____

____

____

____

____

How can you use this to move toward your destiny?

____

____

____

____

____

____

____

· · ·

Your prayer:

CHAPTER TWENTY-FIVE
Z - ZEAL

great enthusiasm or energy in pursuit of a
cause or an objective.

When we become teenagers, we spend a lot of our time thinking about dating—going out with that one special person.

We've become enamored, or smitten, as my grandparents' generation would have said. All we do is think about that person. We wonder what they are doing, where they are, and if they are thinking about us. I remember getting on the phone with that special someone and just listening to them breathe. I know you remember when you ran out of things to say, you just sat there in silence until your parents said it was time to get off the phone. It's pretty funny now that I look back, but when it was happening, I was very serious about that relationship. I had a zeal for that person. They were my sun, moon, and stars.

As we grow older, we still have those feelings about that special someone, but they tend to be more intense. Now we wonder if he will propose. We think, "He says he loves me, so I think it's going to happen soon." Those thoughts begin to run through our minds. We are committed to this relationship 150 percent. The enthusiasm and energy for the relationship are off the charts. Every waking moment is spent thinking and wondering about your true love. Well, before you can fully commit to another person, you should have committed to a relationship with God. That relationship actually prepares you for every other relationship you will have in your lifetime. Your relationship with God is one with your Father. It teaches you the things you need to know to grow and live a life pleasing to Him. He gives you instructions, and He even corrects you when you are wrong, as a parent should. Then there is that relationship with Jesus, who is the groom, and the church is the bride. That is our example of how a strong marriage should be built.

Ephesians 5:25-33 (ESV) says: "Husbands, love your wives, as Christ loved the church and gave himself up for her, that he might sanctify her, having cleansed her by the washing of water with the word, so that he might present the church to himself in splendor, without spot or wrinkle or any such thing, that she might be holy and without blemish. In the same way husbands should love their wives as their own bodies. He who loves his wife loves himself. For no one ever hated his own flesh, but nourishes and cherishes it, just as Christ does the church." The church is us. We the people, not the building. God lives in us, not in the actual building. Christ had love, compassion, and empathy for the people he met. It didn't matter if they were Jews or not. All people were his people. He gave all he had to his bride (us), down to his last drop of blood. Christ was the greatest example of having zeal for others. If only we followed the examples he left for us.

For husbands, this means love your wives, just as Christ loved the church. He gave up his life for her. (Eph. 5:25 NLT)

• • •

Dana's prayer:

God, I come to you now asking for continued direction on the path your son Jesus left as an example for me. Father, I desire to live a life pleasing to you, one full of zest (great enthusiasm and energy) for me and for your people. I pray that my eyes would be open to see how I can be a better bride for my husband according to your word and a better bride to those here in the world. I pray that the compassion, love, and empathy Jesus had for us be shown through us in our daily walk. Just as Jesus simply saw people, I pray that we begin to only see people. Not your ethnicity, not religion, not the way we speak, and not our color. Just see each other as children of the Most High God who loved us all so much, He sacrificed His only son for our lives. God, I give you glory, honor, and praise. I thank you in Jesus's name, Amen.

What are your takeaways?

____

____

____

____

____

____

____

How can you use this to move toward your destiny?

____

____

____

____

____

____

____

· · ·

Your prayer:

About the Author

Dana, known as the Freedom Fighter, is a wife, a mother,

and a Nana of four. She is a coach, a teacher, a motivator, and a speaker. Dana helps people unlock things within them that have hindered them from reaching their goals. She is called to serve women who are broken, who have been abused physically, mentally, and emotionally. To help them gain confidence and see themselves the way God sees them and help move them toward their destiny.

She is a firm believer that you control your destiny, and the first thing to do is take a step. She believes that we hinder ourselves by being afraid. Afraid to fail and afraid to succeed. Dana says that we are in a place called stuck. She also believes there is light at the end of the darkest tunnels if you only open your mind, heart, and spirit to see it.

www.ingramcontent.com/pod-product-compliance
Lightning Source LLC
Chambersburg PA
CBHW061541050726
47593CB00002B/861